ALSO BY MICHAEL RUHLMAN

*The Elements of Cooking*
*The Making of a Chef*
*The Soul of a Chef*
*The Reach of a Chef*

COOKBOOK COLLABORATIONS

*The French Laundry Cookbook*
*A Return to Cooking*
*Bouchon*
*Charcuterie:*
*The Craft of Salting, Smoking and Curing*

GENERAL NONFICTION

*Boys Themselves*
*Wooden Boats*
*Walk on Water*
*House: A Memoir*

# RATIO

*The Simple Codes Behind the Craft*
*of Everyday Cooking*

## MICHAEL RUHLMAN

SCRIBNER

New York   London   Toronto   Sydney

SCRIBNER

A Division of Simon & Schuster, Inc.
1230 Avenue of the Americas
New York, NY 10020

First Scribner trade paperback edition September 2010

SCRIBNER and design are trademarks of The Gale Group, Inc.,
used under license by Simon & Schuster, Inc., the publisher of this work.

For information about special discounts for bulk purchases,
please contact Simon & Schuster Special Sales at
1-866-506-1949 or business@simonandschuster.com.

DESIGNED BY ERICH HOBBING

Text set in Adobe Garamond

Manufactured in the United States of America

1   3   5   7   9   10   8   6   4   2

Library of Congress Control Number: 2008032679

ISBN 978-1-4165-6611-3
ISBN 978-1-4165-7172-8 (pbk)
ISBN 978-1-4165-6612-0 (ebook)

Photographs by Donna Turner Ruhlman

For Uwe Hestnar

# Contents

# The Ratios

## Doughs

Bread = 5 parts flour : 3 parts water (plus yeast and salt)
Pasta Dough = 3 parts flour : 2 parts egg
Pie Dough = 3 parts flour : 2 parts fat : 1 part water
Biscuit = 3 parts flour : 1 part fat : 2 parts liquid
Cookie Dough = 1 part sugar : 2 parts fat : 3 parts flour
*Pâte à Choux* = 2 parts water : 1 part butter : 1 part flour : 2 parts egg

## Batters

Pound Cake = 1 part butter : 1 part sugar : 1 part egg : 1 part flour
Sponge Cake = 1 part egg : 1 part sugar : 1 part flour : 1 part butter
Angel Food Cake = 3 parts egg white : 3 parts sugar : 1 part flour
Quick Bread = 2 parts flour : 2 parts liquid : 1 part egg : 1 part butter
Muffin = 2 parts flour : 2 parts liquid : 1 part egg : 1 part butter
Fritter = 2 parts flour : 2 parts liquid : 1 part egg
Pancake = 2 parts flour : 2 parts liquid : 1 part egg : ½ part butter
Popover = 2 parts liquid : 1 part egg : 1 part flour
Crepe = 1 part liquid : 1 part egg : ½ part flour

## Stocks and Sauces

Stock = 3 parts water : 2 parts bones

Consommé = 12 parts stock : 3 parts meat : 1 part mirepoix : 1 part egg white

Roux = 3 parts flour : 2 parts fat

Thickening Ratio = 10 parts liquid : 1 part roux

*Beurre Manié* = 1 part flour : 1 part butter (by volume)

Slurry = 1 part cornstarch : 1 part water (by volume)

Thickening Rule = 1 tablespoon starch will thicken 1 cup liquid

## Meat

Sausage = 3 parts meat : 1 part fat

Sausage Seasoning = 60 parts meat/fat : 1 part salt

Mousseline = 8 parts meat : 4 parts cream : 1 part egg

Brine = 20 parts water : 1 part salt

## Fat-Based Sauces

Mayonnaise = 20 parts oil : 1 part liquid (plus yolk)

Vinaigrette = 3 parts oil : 1 part vinegar

Hollandaise = 5 parts butter : 1 part yolk : 1 part liquid

## Custards

Free-Standing Custard = 2 parts liquid : 1 part egg

Crème Anglaise = 4 parts milk/cream : 1 part yolk : 1 part sugar

Chocolate Sauce = 1 part chocolate : 1 part cream

Caramel Sauce = 1 part sugar : 1 part cream

# What Is a Ratio
# and Why Is It Important?

A culinary ratio is a fixed proportion of one ingredient or ingredients relative to another. These proportions form the backbone of the craft of cooking. When you know a culinary ratio, it's not like knowing a single recipe, it's instantly knowing a thousand. Here is the ratio for bread: 5 parts flour : 3 parts water.

This means that if you combine 5 ounces of flour and 3 ounces of water, or 20 ounces of flour and 12 ounces of water, or 500 grams of flour and 300 grams of water, you will, if you mix it properly, have a good bread dough. You need a small amount of yeast, but the exact amount is hugely variable as it turns out, so that's not a meaningful part of the ratio. You need salt for flavor, but that is a matter of taste to a large degree. And you need to mix the dough until it has enough elasticity to contain the gas released by the yeast. So while there are rules to follow and issues of technique, these are not part of the ratio.

What can you do, now that you know the bread ratio? You can make fresh bread without opening a single book or scouring a website for random recipes, and you can

*Three of your most valuable tools in the kitchen:* ▶
*flour, eggs, and butter.*

make as much or as little as you like. That 500 grams of flour or 20 ounces of flour with the water, a big pinch of dry yeast, and 2 big pinches of salt make a good loaf of bread. But if you want to liven it up, add a tablespoon of freshly chopped rosemary and a head of roasted garlic and stretch it out for a roasted garlic and rosemary ciabatta. Other fresh herbs such as thyme, sage, and oregano work beautifully, too. Or use other intense, flavorful ingredients: poblano and chipotle peppers, kalamata olives and walnuts, chocolate and cherries, pistachios and cranberries. Caramelized onion! A sausage! Cheese! The variations are limitless because you know the ratio, 5 parts flour, 3 parts water. Eventually you'll feel comfortable using some whole grain flour in there or potato.

Of course, many, many variables contribute to the end result—how long the final rise is, how hot the oven, how well you shaped the dough, and so on—and addressing those variables can make baking feel dauntingly complicated. Indeed, baking that perfect loaf of bread every time takes practice and thoughtfulness; whole books are devoted to it. But on the most basic level, baking bread is not complicated.

Feel like making fresh pizza? Ten ounces of flour, 6 ounces of water, a pinch of yeast, and a pinch of salt will give you dough for a medium pie. Many recipes for pizza dough include a sugar of some kind—if that's to your taste, add a tablespoon of sugar or honey (you'll find this increases yeast activity). Many add a flavoring of olive oil. Go for it. Stick to the 5 : 3 ratio and you're golden.

Want an easy delicious white sandwich bread for the kids? Same ratio (and maybe add some wheat germ for additional fiber and some honey for flavor and sweetness). But still it's 5 to 3. Just cook it more gently, 350°F for an hour or so, until it's very hot inside.

This book is composed of such ratios.

Cooking is infinitely nuanced and there

◀ *All measuring spoons are not alike. Avoid boutiquey, porcelain, plastic, or gimmicky measuring devices.*

are ultimately too many variables to account for in any single recipe (the ambient humidity, how long a bag of flour has been sitting in the cupboard), so it's important to remember, as my first culinary instructor notes, "how well ratios work is directly proportionate to the ratio of common sense applied to them." Good technique must be used in conjunction with the ratio—which is why this is a book and not a sheet of paper. You need the ratio and the user's manual. Technique must be practiced—you can never stop getting better.

This is important: my aim isn't to make the perfect bread or pasta or mayonnaise or biscuits—"the best I've ever had." It's to set a baseline to work from, to codify the fundamentals from which we work and which we work off of. When I was writing *Walk on Water,* about a renowned surgeon, more than one doctor noted the common saying, "great is the enemy of good," meaning that when surgeons strive for greatness, they can cause harm when they might otherwise not have harmed had they simply strived for good. I've worked with the greatest perfectionist there is in the cooking world, and I love that hunt for the perfect sauce, the perfect custard, but here I'm after good. Only when we know good can we begin to inch up from good to excellent.

Here is another thing knowing a ratio does: it helps you to better understand cooking in general. How does bread differ from fresh pasta? Not all that much actually, except that for pasta, egg takes the place of water at a ratio of 3 parts flour and 2 parts egg. What's the difference between bread dough and pie dough? The proportions of flour and water are a little different (3 : 1), but it's the important third ingredient, fat, that makes it pie dough—fat is responsible for making pie dough unlike bread dough, tender rather than chewy. The pie dough ratio is fairly standard: 3 : 2 : 1 (3 parts flour, 2 parts fat, and 1 part water) and it's often referred to as 3-2-1 Pie Dough. It's a great ratio because it's so versatile. It's also possible to make a really bad pie dough using this ratio if you don't know the properties of pie dough and the fact that the gentler you are with it, the more tender it will be. But the ratio itself is bedrock.

The fact is, there are hundreds of thousands of recipes out there, but few of them help you to be a better cook in any substantial way. In fact, they may hurt you as a cook by keeping you chained to recipes. Getting your hands on a ratio is like being given a key to unlock those chains. Ratios free you.

Ratios are about the basics of cooking. They teach us how the fundamental ingredients of the kitchen—flour, water, butter and oils, milk and cream, eggs—work and how variations in proportions create the variations in our dishes, bread rather than pasta, crepes rather than cakes.

Doughs and batters are where ratios really shine because the proportions of the basic ingredients, the ratios, define the end result. When you get right down to it, the main difference between a sweet crepe batter and a sponge cake is that crepe batter has half as much flour.

Other kinds of ratios for fundamental preparations expand your reach in much the same way. Among the most common ratios is that for a standard vinaigrette. Couldn't be simpler: 3 parts oil, 1 part vinegar. That's it. Works great. Stir together and dress some greens. Once you have that, then it only follows that you may want to enhance the flavor a little, add some salt and pepper and, for balance, some sugar. Perhaps some aromatics, fresh herbs, a roasted shallot, brown rather than white sugar, and honey. Perhaps you want it thick and creamy, so you might emulsify it. You might want to change your fat (bacon rather than canola oil, olive rather than bacon) or the acid (sherry vinegar rather than red wine vinegar, lemon juice rather than sherry).

If you know the ratio for a mayonnaise, you don't know just mayonnaise—which is an amazing preparation when you make it yourself (see page 175 for a simple hand-blender version)—you know a creamy lime-cumin dressing for a grilled pork sandwich and you know a lemon-shallot dipping sauce for a steamed artichoke. The elegant hollandaise, a thick butter sauce, becomes a stately béarnaise sauce when you pack it with fresh tarragon. Know the hollandaise ratio and technique rather than a specific recipe for hollandaise sauce, and you can infuse it with chillis, or reduced red wine and rosemary for roasted leg of lamb. There's no end to what you can do in the kitchen when you know a ratio.

Custards, of course, are ratio based and couldn't be simpler: 2 parts liquid (usually but not necessarily milk or cream) and 1 part egg. Large eggs are very close to 2 ounces each, so that works out to 8 ounces of liquid to 2 eggs. More expected for dinner? Make that 16 ounces and 4 eggs. This results in a great crème caramel, but you can go savory if you want—bone marrow and coriander, a savory mint custard for that lamb instead of the butter sauce. How do you know how much mint to add? Using ratios enables you to begin thinking as chefs do; they use their common sense and they taste as they go.

Ratios are even helpful to consider in those preparations that are typically measured by sight, such as making a stock, or thickening a stock for a soup or a sauce. Is there a foundation ratio for stock? Not really, but it's useful for gaining a sense of proper proportions, especially if you're just beginning to cook.

Because dough and batter ratios are so instructive, I'm leading off with those. That section is followed by soups and sauces, where ratios are valuable in different ways. With fat-based sauces, ratios determine the amount of fat used relative to other ingredients. For stocks, and stock-based sauces and soups, ratios are more a guide than a definitive proportion, and they also help us to achieve specific consistencies. Soups and sauces are followed by ratios for sausages and *pâtés,* meat-based ratios, which are in a different realm from those undergirding doughs and batters in that they primarily concern proportions of salt and fat. And I end with custards—among my most favorite things to eat—which can be savory or sweet, solid enough to stand unmolded on their own, others that are voluptuous and creamy, and finally basic dessert sauces, most notable, the remarkable custard sauce.

With the advent of the Internet, we have access to an ocean of recipes but relatively less information on food and cooking. Understanding ratios and technique is, for the home cook, a step toward becoming more independent in the kitchen. But ratios are just as important to chefs and other food professionals because they provide a launching point for the development of new dishes.

Technique will ultimately determine the quality of the end result. Ratios are the points from which infinite variations begin.

# The All-Important Scale

One of the facts underlying the universality of **ratios** is that they are based on **weight** rather than on volume measurements. This is what allows them to be doubled or tripled or halved. It doesn't even matter what unit you're using, grams or ounces. Weighing your ingredients is the best and most consistent form of measuring, and it's the fundamental tool when it comes to using kitchen ratios. Some old ratios use volume measurements or units—1 cup of oil and 1 yolk equal mayonnaise is an example of a common ratio. In most cases, I've avoided these kinds of measurements because they are inconsistent, and instead I have tried wherever possible to use parts by weight. A cup of flour can weigh anywhere between 4 and 6 ounces. This means that if you are making a recipe calling for 4 cups of flour, you might wind up with a pound of flour in your bowl or you might end up with 1½ pounds. That's a 50 percent difference in the main ingredient, which will have a substantial impact on the finished product. Using parts by weight in these ratios also ensures that it doesn't matter what kind of measurements you use, imperial or metric—5 parts flour and 3 parts

*A scale is one of the most important tools in the ▶ kitchen. Be sure the scale you buy can measure food weighing up to 5 pounds, has a zeroing or tare button, and can measure in metric and imperial weights.*

liquid can be measured either way. Of course, the weight of flour can be affected by humidity—the greater the humidity, the more moisture in your flour—but ratios by weight remains the most consistent way to measure.

Using a scale also simplifies your life. You can measure ingredients right into your bowl. To take the bread example, you might simply put your mixing bowl on the scale, pour in flour until you have 20 ounces, then pour in 12 ounces of water. If you're using solid fat such as shortening for a pie dough, using a scale is much cleaner. I've always been annoyed by recipes that call for a cup of shortening. It's so much easier to set your mixing bowl on the scale and spoon in 8 ounces (which will be a little more than a cup in volume) with your 12 ounces of flour.

That being said, there is still reason to use volume measurements for some solid ingredients, the biggest of which is convenience. When precision is not critical, volume measurements are acceptable. If you were adding freshly cut corn to bread, for instance, or fresh herbs, it's easier to measure out a cup of corn than 5 ounces, a quarter cup of herbs than .5 ounces. In such cases, I use volume measurements.

For small measurements of uniform ingredients, such as dry yeast or baking powder, I use teaspoon and tablespoon measures. This is why the ratios for *beurre manié* (a flour-butter thickener) and slurry (a pure starch and water thickener) are by volume, not weight.

All other ratios are by weight and are best measured with a scale. Most of the dough and batter ratios include flour. If you do not have a scale, assume that a level cup of flour weighs about 5 ounces or 140 grams.

There are many kinds of scales. I recommend your scale have a few specific features. It should be digital, it should be able to measure in both grams and ounces, and it should be able to read up to 5 pounds or more. Other features, as far as I'm concerned, are superfluous and a matter of personal preference. Good digital scales are available starting at about $25 and are one of the most important tools in the kitchen.

# Using This Book

This book is about the culinary fundamentals, without which, as Escoffier said, nothing of importance can be accomplished. Nothing. But because it's about the fundamentals, it's also about all the things you can do with those fundamentals, about variation and improvisation. While it's filled with recipes, I like to think of it as an anti-recipe book, a book that teaches you and frees you from the need to follow.

All ratios are listed in the order that the ingredients are combined. That is, a 3-2-1 pie dough means that flour is the first ingredient, fat is added to the flour and mixed in, then water is added.

Is a scale required? No. I've tried to make every recipe and ratio accessible to those who don't have a scale. It's mainly a flour issue. Most of the fundamental ingredients have built-in units. A large egg is 2 ounces. A stick of butter is 4. A cup of water or cream or milk is 8 ounces. So in terms of measuring, flour is the one primary ingredient whose weight varies from cup to cup. So for those not using a scale, figure a cup weighs between 4 and 6 ounces. So for a 3-2-1 pie dough, you'd use a cup of flour, a stick of butter, and ¼ cup of water (keeping in mind you may need to add a little more flour). But again, scales make kitchen life so much easier.

## A Note to Culinary Professionals

I hope you'll find the fundamental ratios valuable as a quick reference in your own endlessly variable and creative endeavors. Do note that these recipes have been tested for home proportions, not for production quantities. Because they're weight based, they should work well when scaled up, but the higher you go, the more tweaking may be necessary, especially when chemical leaveners are involved. I haven't made a batter for 50 angel food cakes or crepes for 500. My sense, though, is that as you move into high-volume production, small variables, such as ambient humidity, can become big variables.

## Notes About the Fundamental Ingredients

- "Flour" means all-purpose flour unless otherwise noted.
- "Salt" means coarse kosher salt. (I use Morton's kosher salt, which has a close volume-to-weight ratio; that is, a tablespoon equals ½ ounce.)
- "Eggs" means large eggs, which weigh about 2 ounces.
- "Butter" can mean salted or sweet, whichever is your preference, unless noted in the recipe. Most chefs prefer to use sweet because it has a purer flavor and it allows them to better control the salt level of their food. I prefer the flavor of salted butter in most, not all, preparations; it's what I'm used to in terms of seasoning food. Regardless of your butter preference, you should always season to taste. When butter is a predominant component of a ratio, as with the 1–2–3 cookie ratio, it should go without saying that the better the butter, the better the cookie.

# Introduction:
# The Truth of Cooking

My first impressions of Uwe Hestnar are of mystery, inscrutability. A chef at the Culinary Institute of America (CIA) who hails from Hamburg, Germany, Hestnar has moved up into administration and out of the classroom. As a dean he makes brief silent appearances in my Skills class, culinary basics, at the school. I'll keep an eye on him—he's like a spy, I assume dangerous. Big, forceful-looking, with square features and a thick accent. One minute he's there, the next he's gone. As I mince my onion and concassé my tomato, I spot him over by the giant steam kettle peering into it. He dips a soup bowl in the veal stock, lifts it out, and stares at it as he lets the stock drain off it. When Chef Hestnar is speaking with my instructor, I approach them with my peas and pearl onions (vegetable cookery) for judgment. They quickly stop speaking. My instructor tastes and comments and Hestnar also asks to taste. "Too crunchy?" I ask him. "He's the chef," Hestnar says, not looking at me.

*Some ladles double as measuring devices, such as ▶ these 2- and 8-ounce ladles. I recommend owning a 2-ounce, a 4-ounce, and an 8-ounce ladle for both easy measuring and even portioning when you're using them to serve.*

I make an appointment to meet him, to interview him for the book I'm writing, because I find him so mysterious. The encounter is transformative. It is the seed of this book.

Seated in his small office, I tell him I've come to the school to write about the basics of cooking. He says, "Za fundamentals of cooking don't change." And the way he says it carries such gravity, the sentence seems to extend all the way back to the origins of cooking itself, to the moment Homo sapiens first applied heat to food because food tasted better that way.

We talk about how one learns to cook and what the culinary arts are all about. He is dismissive of recipes with lots of ingredients. What impresses him is a really good cheese sauce.

"People don't want to pay five dollars for two ingredients," he says. He says that a dish with twenty ingredients is not the sign of a good cook because mistakes are too easy to cover. Cauliflower with cheese sauce is the true test of a chef.

"The shelves are bulging with cookbooks," he says derisively.

"You don't like that?" I ask.

He says that everything a cook needs to know—*everything,* mind you—is contained in five books: Escoffier, Larousse, Hering's Dictionary, *La Repetoire.* I tell him that's only four. "And Câreme," he says. He pauses. "No one wants."

As I will write in *The Making of a Chef,* he then asks, "What makes the culinary arts tick?"

I don't know if he's actually directing this to me or offering it rhetorically. He has more or less lofted it into the air. He lifts his index finger, then spins in his chair to a file behind him, as if quickly reaching for a bat to knock the question into the bleachers. He riffles manila folders and turns to me with two sheets of paper. They contain a chart or grid covering a page and a half. This, he says, is all one truly needs. Here are the fundamentals of the culinary arts—all of Escoffier, Larousse, Câreme, as well as Julia Child, James Beard, *The Joy of Cooking,* and the Food Network—in their entirety, distilled to a page and a half. "I vould like to zell *this* for fifty dollars," he says, "but no one vould buy." Then he chuckles heartily, rocking in his chair.

I examine the sheets—a list of twenty-six items and their ratios. Along the top run the numbers 1, 2, 4, 6, 8, and 16. Along the side are rows divided by base products such as aspic, *pâte à choux,* sabayon, court bouillon ordinaire. A primitive culinary spreadsheet.

I find this document mysteriously thrilling. For hollandaise sauce, the sheet lists "lbs. butter" in the 1 column and "egg yolks" in the 6 column. One pound of butter, 6 egg yolks, nothing more. We had learned to make hollandaise sauce in Skills class by reducing cider vinegar with cracked pepper and adding this, strained and with lemon juice, to yolks we'd cooked frothy and into which we'd whip clarified butter. But on Chef Hestnar's grid of ratios, he has reduced the classic butter sauce to its essence. Take away vinegar, pepper, and lemon and you still have hollandaise. Take away yolks or butter and it ceased to be hollandaise.

I find the ratio sheet beautiful. Like a poet chipping away at his words, compressing and polishing until his idea is a diamond, Hestnar has removed every extraneous element of cooking.

I ask if I can hang on to the ratios and thank him.

I keep them in a folder. I stare at them every now and then. After my book is published in 1997, readers write to ask for a copy and I send it to them. I ask a friend who has an artful hand, Caryn, to copy out the ratios so that I can frame them. Caryn thinks that I should note something more than "Kitchen Ratios" in the heading. I think about it and say, "'A History of Cooking.'" Because that's exactly what they represent to me, and more. The *truth* of cooking. All that is unchanging, fixed, elemental.

This book is an exploration of that idea, fundamental kitchen ratios that all cooks might share.

When I begin to evaluate Hestnar's ratios, I discover much to disagree with. For stock, he has equal parts bones and water, not nearly enough water in my pots. His custard, I believe, may include more

*A chinois is a conical, fine-mesh strainer used* ▶
*not only to strain but also to create a fine texture.*

egg than one really needs. His hollandaise ratio is practically universal in all cookbooks, but do you really need 6 yolks for a pound of butter, given that for a mayonnaise the ratio calls for 2 yolks for the same quantity of fat?

Only a fool has the arrogance to be dogmatic about cooking, which is infinitely variable, but why can't there be a standard from which all cooks begin?

As I prepare to write this book, I reach Hestnar on his cell. He is retired and living on a boat off the coast of Virginia at the time. He sounds delighted to talk again about ratios. Where did the ratios come from? I ask. Who put them together, and why? He explains that he did. He was teaching Skills classes, he says, and it drove him crazy that his students had to keep opening books and burying their faces in recipes while cooking. They weren't understanding that cooking was not about recipes but rather about fundamental techniques and basic ratios of the way food came together. So he simply went to his main texts, compared various recipes, and came up with his ratios.

It occurs to me that since I left the Culinary Institute of America, I've been trying to bring both the ethos and the lessons of the professional kitchen to the home kitchen, to make home cooks familiar with all the knowledge common to professional cooks. Ratios is one of the greatest cooking lessons there is. Again, technique is a fundamental part of the equation, but ratios open up worlds. They turn once complicated procedures, like cake making or bread baking, into simple pleasures. They allow you to close the book and cook as you wish. They free you.

One of my favorite ratios is 3-2-1 Pie Dough. I like it because I'm not a pastry cook, but for this pastry procedure, I don't have to open a book—I know the recipe, 3-2-1: 3 parts flour, 2 parts fat, 1 part water; and the method: combine 3 and 2, then add 1 (12 ounces flour, 8 ounces shortening or butter, 4 ounces cold water—perfect for a single pie shell and top or 2 tart shells).

My friend and former CIA instructor Bob del Grosso loves the 1-2-3 cookie dough because, he says, with no seasoning, 1 part sugar, 2 parts fat, followed by 3 parts flour will produce a basic short cookie. "It won't be art," he says, "but it will be good." Add vanilla or chocolate, lemon and poppy seeds, choose a very flavorful butter—that's the art. Hollandaise is butter emulsified into yolks. The pepper, the lemon juice, the cider reduction, that's the art part.

But even in studying these tried-and-true ratios, I find there is much to learn. You really don't need all that yolk in a hollandaise to maintain the emulsification, what you really do need, though, is water. So I would need to make water part of the ratio (see page 185).

Do we really need ratios for stocks? No, and certainly not after you've made them a few times. You should measure by sight and experience. But here a ratio is a good benchmark to learn from. And thickening those stocks for soups and sauces is useful, especially for those learning to cook. So the stock chapter covers a lot of basic terms and techniques.

The fat-based sauces, mayonnaise, hollandaise and its derivatives, and the vinaigrette—one of the most versatile and important sauces there is—as well as custards, are all based on a ratio of fat to the rest of the ingredients, as are forcemeats, sausages, and *pâtés*. Custard, too, is a kind of fat-based sauce that benefits from ratios.

But I'm opening this book with doughs and batters because these are where ratios really shine and help any kind of cook, from novice to expert, understand the way the fundamental building blocks of cuisine, flour, water, and eggs behave given varying proportions of each. Indeed there is a dough-batter continuum that runs from thick and elastic to thin and delicate to soft to pourable that became a revelation to me when viewed through the lens of ratios.

We must have craft before we have art, and craft is founded on fundamentals. I've long wanted to quantify and explore these fundamentals. And so I set out to write this book.

*Butcher's string is a handy tool to have in the ▶ kitchen—for tying meats so that they cook uniformly and look good; for tying up hard herbs to be added to stews and soups and then removed from the pot; and for tying sachets, herbs, and spices in cheesecloth, to season soups, stews, and braises.*

# PART ONE

# Doughs and Batters

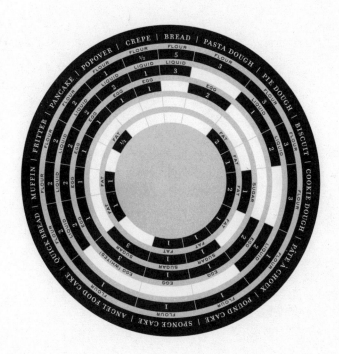

# DOUGHS

Dough almost invariably signifies some form of ground cereal grain held together with some form of moisture. The simplest dough is flour and water, and will be relatively flavorless unless you do something to it, such as add fat, egg, yeast, salt, sugar, or if you wrap it around something tasty (ground pork) and fry it, as with a Chinese pot sticker (6 tablespoons of cold water into a cup of flour will give you a workable pot sticker dough, or about 2 to 1 by weight). Adding fat "shortens" the dough—that is, shortens the strands of gluten that make a dough chewy. Fat is the difference between a noodle dough and a crumbly pastry dough. Eggs enrich a dough, whether fat is included or not. Yeast both leavens dough (a dough with fat, such as brioche, or without fat, such as a baguette) and gives it flavor. Sugar sweetens a dough, as in a traditional *pâte sucrée*. And salt does many things to a dough—for instance, it can inhibit the growth of yeast or bacteria in naturally fermented doughs, it can tighten the gluten network and make a dough more elastic, and, of course, it enhances flavor. Doughs can be the feature attraction (bread, pasta, cookie) or a vehicle for other tastes and textures (tarts, savory and sweet pies, and dumplings).

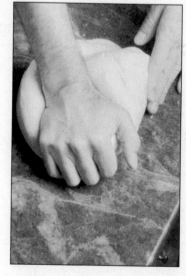

# Bread Dough

## Bread = 5 parts flour : 3 parts water (plus yeast and salt)

Everyone should be able to make bread when they want to, but rarely do we because of the perceived effort involved. When you know the ratio for bread, bread is easy. You don't need a recipe or even a measuring cup. All you need is a bowl and a scale. The bread ratio is a common one. I've adapted it from what is called the baker's percentage: 100 percent flour, 60 percent water, 3 percent fresh yeast, 2 percent salt. It's a good working ratio. If you want more bread, double it. If your scale has a gram measurement on it, it's even easier (and shows why metric weights are so much more efficient than our U.S. equivalents): 1,000 grams of flour, 600 grams of water, 30 grams of fresh yeast, 20 grams of salt. If you have a standing mixer, your dough can be mixing in a matter of minutes. Set your mixing bowl on the scale, zero it out, add your flour; zero the scale again and add your water; add the yeast to the water to make sure it dissolves, add the salt, and begin mixing.

Yeast and salt are critical components in basic bread dough, but they are used in such small quantities that making them part of the ratio makes the ratio more complicated than I think it needs to be. Salt is critical for flavor. Bread tastes bland without it. The baker's percentage calls for 2 percent of the weight of the flour. So you can measure it that way if you wish: .2 ounces for every 10 ounces of flour, or 2 grams for every 100 grams of flour. This is where a scale really comes in handy, but if you measure only by volume, you can add ¼ teaspoon of kosher salt for every cup of flour, or 1 teaspoon for 4 cups (which usually weighs about 20 ounces).

Yeast, of course, is what makes bread such a pleasure to eat. But it's also mysterious—the yeast organisms are alive but invisible. Yeast comes in numerous forms—fresh, active, and instant—and this can be confusing. Active yeast? When would you want *inactive* yeast? What's the difference between active and instant? Why would you use fresh?

I learned bread baking with fresh yeast: perishable, fragrant cakes with a wonderful and unique texture that turn to a paste in the liquid and dissolve. I've found that using fresh yeast results in the best flavor for basic white hearth bread, also called a lean bread or lean dough, as opposed to a soft white bread that includes fats, sugar, or egg. But bakers increasingly use dried yeast because of increased quality and a longer shelf life. I now use Red Star yeast, and many bakers use SAF yeast (also the maker of Red Star yeast) for its performance and flavor.

Active dry yeast is yeast that's been dried and given an inactive coating; this yeast must be dissolved in water before being mixed with the flour. Most companies recommend doing this in water that's about 110°F. But this seems to be for insurance rather than a strict requirement. I add mine to cold water and it's always worked fine. Instant, or quick-rise, yeast has been quickly dried and doesn't have the same coating on it, and so does not need to be rehydrated before being added to the water and flour.

Instant comes as smaller granules and, because it doesn't consist partially of inactive yeast, is the stronger of the two yeasts by weight. Active dry yeast is typically soaked first, instant does not need to be. Yeast can be stored in the refrigerator but is best stored in the freezer.

The quantity of dried yeast you need to raise a loaf of bread is remarkably variable regardless of the type. Adding ¼ teaspoon, ½ teaspoon (2 grams), or 2½ teaspoons will result in similar leavening. The more yeast, the faster it goes, and as a rule, the longer the fermentation time (time during which the yeast feeds and releases gas), the more flavorful the bread. A bread that's mixed with a lot of yeast and baked 4 hours later hasn't had the time to develop flavors—so adding flavors to these doughs, herbs, aromatics, olives, nuts, even a coating of olive oil and coarse salt before baking, goes a long way in this case. It's a good strategy, though, to mix the dough a day ahead and allow it to ferment in the refrigerator for a day, then let it sit out to warm slightly before baking it. Most manufacturers suggest how much yeast will leaven a given amount of flour—2¼ ounces will leaven 4 cups of flour, for instance. But ⅛ teaspoon, ¼ gram, will leaven that same amount of flour given enough time (and result in a better flavor from the increased fermentation). Adding too much yeast will cause the dough to rise too quickly and it won't develop any flavor, though if you're in a hurry, adding too much yeast works. As a rule, either follow the instructions on the package or add 1 teaspoon for every pound of flour, which is about 3 cups. If you prefer to use fresh yeast, calculate your yeast quantity by multiplying the weight of your flour by .03. But, again, the other elements of making the dough are more critical than the type or amount of yeast used.

Bread is alive until you cook it, and so it's an especially complex system that's affected by many variables, especially temperature, but also by how long it's mixed, how long it rises, how long it rises again before being baked, and how it's shaped. All these variables affect the finished bread, so you need to pay attention as you practice. And mastering these variables, bringing bread baking to the artisan level, takes time and requires special ovens, varying mixtures of flour, the use of wild yeasts for sourdoughs, or prefermenting part of the bread—creating what's called a sponge, or using dough left over from a previous batch, often called a *levain*. But the fact is, the baseline for a good bread dough is the baker's percentage or, simplified, 5 : 3 flour to water. It's good as is, but because you're not developing flavor through the above techniques of long fermentation and natural yeast starters, it's best to give it a little extra flavor by rubbing it with olive oil and giving it a sprinkling of salt before it goes into the oven.

Bread basics are important. Mixing the flour-water-yeast combination is the first critical step. Mixing or kneading develops the gluten, the protein in flour that results in a dough's becoming elastic. A standing mixer and a dough hook make the mixing very easy, but remember that it's possible to overmix a dough with a mixer—the gluten network can break down after too much mixing, resulting in a flabby dough that doesn't hold the gas bubbles well. It's difficult to overmix when kneading by hand. You've mixed your dough enough when you can stretch a small piece of it into a translucent sheet without tearing it.

Elasticity is the quality that allows a dough to be leavened. As the yeast feeds and releases gas, the dough stretches but is strong enough to contain the bubbles. The first rise allows the yeast to multiply and feed and release

◀ *The windowpane test. To know if you've kneaded your bread dough enough, cut a small piece of it and stretch it gently. If it reaches the point of translucency before it tears, the dough is ready to be shaped into a boule, covered, and left to rise.*

gas (carbon dioxide and ethanol), which helps to flavor the dough as well as to develop the gluten network. Some of the gas is then pressed out of the dough when it's kneaded down after the first rise and shaped, a process that continues to develop gluten structure, release excess gas, and redistribute the yeast to give it a fresh food supply, an important step.

The purpose of allowing the dough to rise is, like mixing, to continue to develop the protein network that gives the dough its wonderful texture. The rises also help to develop flavor, especially with naturally leavened bread, sourdough flavored by wild yeasts and acid-producing bacteria. Bread should be allowed to rise at room temperature (the warmer it is, the faster it will rise) until it's doubled in size. It is then punched down, shaped, allowed to rise again, and then baked. Or it can be refrigerated for up to a day and allowed to temper for an hour or two out of the refrigerator before being baked.

Shaping is the final part of mixing, taking that gluten network and putting it into its final order, whether it's a hand-rolled baguette, which is essentially a rectangle of dough that's folded over and over on itself and then rolled, or simply stretched into a loose shape of a "slipper," or *ciabatta* in Italian. The bread is then allowed to rise again in its final shape, a stage called proofing, for about an hour, depending on the environment. Before cooking the bread, score it with a sharp knife or razor, which helps it to expand and gives it an intriguing appearance. (For ciabatta, don't score it; stipple it aggressively with your fingers.)

The oven environment is important. Professional deck ovens often are built with the capacity to inject steam into the oven during the first minutes of baking. Steam helps to develop an especially delicious crispy crust. Home bakers develop their own strategies for introducing steam or simply moisture into their ovens. Place a cast-iron pan in the oven when you preheat it, then when you put the bread in the oven, you can add a cup of water to this pan to create steam. You can bake your bread in a covered Dutch oven, which traps the water vapor the bread releases during cooking—an exceptional method (see page 13). This can indeed help you to achieve a thick crisp crust, but it's not strictly necessary. And you can bake on a metal baking sheet, but some sort of ceramic cooking surface is best.

When the dough is put into the oven, two things happen. The yeast becomes especially active, generating more gas more quickly, and the gas bubbles that have been created expand with the heat. This creates what is referred to as "oven spring," the rapid growth of the dough during its first minutes in the oven. The yeast activity and gas expansion continue until the heat kills the yeast and solidifies the starch and protein.

Knowing when bread is done comes with experience. When you tap the bottom it should sound hollow; use your common sense; and, if you want, use a thermometer—breads should be at least 165°F internal temperature but ideally are between 180°F and 210°F inside.

A word about flour. Use bread flour for making bread. It has a higher gluten content than all-purpose flour. But if you only have all-purpose flour, use it. It makes good bread, too.

Finally, a reiteration of the convenience of using a scale. When you use a scale, you can measure your flour and water ingredients straight into your mixing bowl; when you're done, the mixing bowl will be the vessel you let your dough rise in, and you'll always get consistent results.

### Basic Bread Dough

The following recipe is what's referred to in bakeshops as a basic lean dough. Meaning there's no fat in it. It's pure bread and it's satisfying and delicious, especially sprinkled with salt and drizzled with olive oil. It can be shaped into a baguette or a boule or stretched into the shape called ciabatta. If shaping it into a boule, I highly recommend cooking it in a Dutch oven (see page 13). And it can be varied in countless ways, a few of which I describe here.

*20 ounces bread flour (about 4 cups)*
*12 ounces water*
*2 teaspoons salt*
*1 teaspoon active or instant yeast*

Set your mixing bowl on a scale (if using), zero the scale, and pour the flour in. Zero the scale again and add the water. Add the salt. Sprinkle the yeast over the surface of the water to allow it to dissolve. Fit the bowl into the mixer and, using the paddle attachment, mix on medium speed until the dough has come together. Replace the paddle with a dough hook. (The whole procedure can be done with a dough hook, but the paddle brings the ingredients together rapidly. This dough can be kneaded by hand as well.) Continue mixing until your dough is smooth and elastic, about 10 minutes. To test your dough, pull off a chunk and stretch it into a square. If it's elastic enough to allow you to achieve a translucent sheet of dough, it's ready. If it tears before you can do this, continue mixing, either in the mixer or by hand, until the dough is smooth and elastic.

Remove the mixing bowl from the machine, cover it with plastic wrap, and allow the dough to rise to about twice its size. Push a finger into the dough. The dough should give some resistance, but not spring back. If it springs back, let it rest longer. If you let your dough rise for too long, it will feel flabby and loose when you press a finger into it and will be less eager to rise when you bake it.

If baking it the same day, preheat your oven to 450°F (preferably 45 minutes before baking). If you intend to use steam, put a cast-iron pan in the oven and add 1 cup water when ready to bake.

Turn the dough out onto a floured surface and knead it to expel excess gas and redistribute the yeast. Cover with a dish towel and let rest for 10 to 15 minutes. Shape the dough into a boule by pushing the dough back and forth on the counter in a circular motion until you have a round smooth ball; or shape it into a ciabatta by pulling it lengthwise so that it's about a foot long and an inch thick. For a baguette, stretch the dough into a rectangle roughly 12 by 6 inches; fold the top edge of the dough over on itself and pound the heel of your hand to pinch this edge down; fold it again, pounding the heel of your palm down to seal it, and continue until it is a roll; then roll by hand and stretch the baguette out as you do so to tighten its interior structure. Cover the dough with a dish towel and allow to rise, or proof, for about an hour. Or cover the dough with plastic wrap and refrigerate for up to a day; allow the bread to rise at room temperature for at least 1½ hours before baking. When ready to bake a boule, slice an X or a pound symbol into the top of the dough to help it to expand; for ciabatta, stipple the dough with your fingers and, if you wish, coat with olive oil and a sprinkling of kosher salt. For a baguette, make long diagonal scores. Bake for 10 minutes at 450°F, then reduce the oven temperature to 375°F and continue baking until done, 45 to 50 minutes for a boule or baguette, 30 minutes for ciabatta.

YIELD: 1 STANDARD LOAF

## What You Can Do Now That You Have the Bread Dough Ratio

Just the plain dough results in good fresh bread no matter how it's shaped, whether into a boule, stretched long and thin, or rolled into a tight tube for a baguette shape. But I find it's best to coat it with some olive oil and a little coarse salt before baking it. And my favorite shape for these simple, quickly made doughs is the ciabatta, primarily because it results in a lot of surface area, which when coated with olive oil and salted, is very tasty. So that's the method I use most for quick bread at home. But once you embrace the bread dough ratio, there's no end to the kinds of breads you can make. Here are a few of the ways you can take advantage of the ratio. The variations all follow the basic bread method: mix the dough till you can achieve the appropriate elasticity, allow it to rise, punch it down, let it rest for 10 minutes or so, then shape it, allow it to rise one last time, and bake it.

- *Olive-walnut bread.* One of the standard breads I did in culinary school included a garnish of chopped kalamata olives and walnuts, a great combination that results in a purple shade and tangy, nutty flavor. Add 1 cup of chopped kalamata olives and ¾ cup roughly chopped walnuts to the basic bread dough midway through mixing. Let rise, shape, and cook as described in the basic bread dough recipe. These breads were typically baked in the ciabatta shape.

- *Rosemary and roasted garlic bread.* Hard herbs, such as thyme, rosemary, and oregano work well in breads and any could be used here. Roast a head of garlic, wrapped in foil with a tablespoon of olive oil, at 350°F for 20 minutes or until tender. Pop the cloves out of their skins and use whole or give them a rough chop. Add them to the dough along with 1½ tablespoons of chopped rosemary or whatever herb you prefer. Stretch the dough into a ciabatta shape and allow it to rise. When ready to bake, stipple it with your fingers. Rub the dough with olive oil and sprinkle with coarse salt before baking.
- *Sage and brown butter bread.* Sage and brown butter is a classic pairing and works great in bread as well. Sauté ½ cup of loosely packed sage leaves, chopped, in 4 ounces of butter until the leaves are crisp and the butter is brown. Put the bottom of the pan into a larger pan full of cold water to stop the cooking. While the butter is still pourable but not hot, mix the dough, reducing the water by 2 ounces, and add the butter and herbs to the bowl after the dough has come together.
- *Chocolate-cherry bread.* Another favorite from culinary school, where students in Richard Coppedge's bread-baking class used a sourdough to contain this garnish of chocolate and dried cherries. But a straight lean dough works beautifully as well. Add 3 ounces of coarsely chopped semisweet or bittersweet chocolate and ¼ cup of dried cherries to the dough halfway through mixing. Shape the dough into a boule, which allows the least surface area and, therefore, the least amount of chocolate on the outside. The loaf is dense and sweet and delicious.
- *Jalapeño and corn focaccia.* Add ⅓ cup of small-diced jalapeño peppers and 1½ cups of fresh corn to the basic bread dough while mixing. Pull into the shape of a disk, finger-stipple the dough, brush it with olive oil, and sprinkle with coarse salt before baking.
- *Grilled focaccia.* Make the focaccia, replacing the jalapeños above with 2 tablespoons chipotles in adobo sauce, 2 to 5 of them depending on how much heat you want (discard the seeds, chop them finely). Instead of baking it, grill the bread over a medium-hot bed of charcoal or wood coals, covered.
- *Onion ciabatta.* Thinly slice 2 Spanish onions and sauté them slowly in olive oil until they are completely browned. Allow them

to cool. Spread the onions over a ciabatta-shaped loaf before cooking, sprinkle ¼ cup of grated Parmigiano-Reggiano over the
onions, and bake as directed.

- *Fried garlic bread.* Add 2 tablespoons of finely minced garlic to the
basic bread dough. Shape into small balls or mini ciabattas after
the first rise, allow to rise again for 45 minutes, and deep-fry in
325°F oil. Best eaten as soon as they're cooked.

- *Flat bread with thyme, olive oil, and kosher salt.* Reduce the yeast by
half and add 1 ounce of olive oil to the basic bread dough. Shape
the dough into small balls the size of a golf ball, flatten them, and
let them rest for 10 minutes; roll them out as flat as you can on a
floured board or countertop, brush with olive oil, and sprinkle
them with fresh-picked thyme and coarse salt. Bake in a 400°F
oven until done, 10 minutes or so, or to taste (more for crispy, less
for chewy). You can bake this in one sheet or, for flatter, cracker-
like bread, cut into 5-inch-wide strips. You can also sprinkle flat
bread dough with sesame seeds or poppy seeds.

- *Pizza dough.* Reduce the yeast by half and add 1 ounce of olive oil
to the basic bread dough. Roll out to the desired thickness. Let rest
beneath a kitchen towel for 10 minutes if you're having trouble
getting it as thin as you wish, then continue to roll it out.

- *White sandwich bread.* Add 2 tablespoons of honey (and ¼ cup
wheat germ for fiber) to the basic bread dough recipe; bake the
dough in a standard, oiled loaf pan at 350°F for an hour, or until
it reaches an internal temperature of 200°F. A bread dough using
15 ounces of flour (and therefore 9 ounces of water) will fill a 9-inch
loaf pan. For a higher-fiber bread, use half whole-wheat flour, half
bread flour. Score lengthwise down the center of the dough before
baking. Brush the top with egg wash halfway through cooking for
an appealing brown crust.

- *Dutch oven method.* Instead of baking your bread on a sheet tray or
a baking stone, bake it in an enamel cast-iron Dutch oven, lid on
for the first 30 minutes, lid off for the remainder of the cooking
time. (Marlene, the lead tester for this book, likes to add 1 tablespoon of honey and 1 or 2 tablespoons of olive oil to the basic
bread dough ingredients.)

I first read about baking bread in a pot in a *New York Times* article about Jim Lahey, who owns Sullivan St Bakery in Manhattan. The article was about his "no-knead" bread—I'm not sure what the value of no-kneading is. But baking the bread in a Dutch oven! What a simple and ingenious idea! That, to me, should amount to a small revolution in home bread baking. It eliminates the need for a baking stone and all the shenanigans of getting steam into a home oven. In the confined area of the Dutch oven, the moisture released by the bread has the same effect as professional deck ovens with steam injection. I'm sure it would work in a large pot with a lid, but enameled cast iron holds heat very well, so the Dutch oven is the preferred vessel.

The best shape for baking in a Dutch oven is the boule, and there are two ways to bake this boule. After mixing and the first rise, the subsequent pounding down and shaping, the dough can be proofed outside the pot or in the pot. If you want to proof the dough outside the pot, I recommend preheating the Dutch oven. But I prefer proofing the boule in the Dutch oven (to avoid having the bread stick, be sure to oil the bottom of the pan first, something you do not need to do if baking in a preheated Dutch oven). I prefer this method because you don't disturb the structure you've created in the final rise and it results in bread with a light, airy crumb.

Preheat your oven to 450°F. When the dough has risen, add a coating of olive oil and some coarse salt, score it with an X, cover the pan, and pop it in the oven. Bake it for ½ hour, then remove the lid and continue baking until done (an internal temperature of 200°F to 210°F), another 15 to 30 minutes. For the basic bread dough, use a 5½- to 7½-quart Dutch oven.

# Pasta Dough

## Pasta Dough = 3 parts flour : 2 parts egg

While there are numerous pasta dough recipes, and while many chefs simply mix by sight, a 3 : 2 ratio of flour to egg works perfectly every time. If you have a scale, here is how easy it is: set a bowl on the scale, add an egg for every full serving you want to make, then add 1½ that weight in flour. So if you're making two full portions, use 2 large eggs (about 4 ounces) and add 6 ounces of flour. If you're making dinner for six, 6 eggs (about 12 ounces) and 18 ounces of flour.

The 3 parts flour, 2 parts egg ratio always works. If the weather is extremely humid or if you store your flour in the freezer, the dough may be a little sticky, in which case you should add a little flour. If you can find 00 flour, Italian flour of a very fine grind, it results in a wonderful texture, but all-purpose flour works great as well. The ratio is golden.

If you don't have a scale, standard volume ratios work fine to a point. Most common volume ratios are 3 to 4 eggs for every 2 cups of flour, but I prefer Marcella Hazan's ratio of 2 eggs per 1 cup of flour, a good alternate ratio if you find yourself scaleless.

Another way to achieve the pasta dough

*When cutting thin strands of pasta, here tagliolini,* ▶ *be sure your dough is well floured, or the strands may stick together once they've passed through the blades.*

you prefer every time is to remember that large eggs weigh about 2 ounces each and a cup of flour typically weighs 5 ounces, so if you were making a 3-egg pasta, you would know to use a scant 2 cups of flour.

No matter how you do it, whether by weight or eggs per cup, making your own fresh pasta is not difficult to do and results in flavorful noodles with a unique texture, delicate but strong, far different from dried pasta. Also, pasta dough is a joy to work with—indeed, many chefs say that of all the tasks they perform in the kitchen, their favorite is making pasta. It forces you to slow down, to think, and the feel of the dough provides a great tactile pleasure.

As with bread dough, the most important part of pasta making is the kneading, the aligning of the gluten network that gives you the texture and elasticity that you want. (There are two schools of thought on how this is achieved, both of which I'll describe, and both of which work well. One, described below, is achieved via kneading, the other, described in Rich Egg Yolk Pasta, page 21, via as little kneading as possible, with the idea that you allow the rollers to do the kneading. It's a matter of personal preference.) Pasta dough should always be kneaded by hand, and this takes a little time. You can mix the egg and flour in a food processor, but the blade cuts, so if you choose this method, you still must develop the gluten by hand; use the machine only to incorporate ingredients, which is just as easy to do by hand for smaller quantities and doesn't leave you with a food processor bowl and blade to clean. For larger quantities, a standing mixer with a dough hook works well. But, again, kneading is the critical point in making pasta. Happily, kneading by hand is fun to do, meditative, and stress releasing. Appreciate the texture of the dough—there's nothing else quite like it. You can feel the dough changing as you work it, growing increasingly smooth as the gluten aligns, until it has almost a velvetlike texture. Pasta dough may be one of the best products to work in your hands, from a purely textural standpoint.

You can roll dough on a floured surface, let it dry a little, then roll it up and slice it as you would a chiffonade—a good way to make the wide pasta such as pappardelle—but a pasta machine with rollers is the best from a standpoint of efficiency and quality. Remember that rolling your dough is still part of the kneading process. You can't rush it. The dough has a spirit of its own and can only be pushed so hard. To ensure the dough reaches the full width of the roller, I cut the following dough into 4 or 5 ¼-pound pieces and roll each one on the largest setting, then fold these pieces in thirds, turn them sideways so that the widest edge is on the roller, and reroll through the largest setting. I then put each piece through each setting once, down to the penultimate setting or the final setting.

As for the home appliances that mix and extrude pasta, Hazan's comments in her book are wise: "Do not be tempted by one of those awful devices that masticate eggs and flour at one end and extrude a choice of pasta shapes through the other end. What emerges is a mucilaginous and totally contemptible product, and moreover, the contraption is a nuisance to clean."

Basic pasta dough, like a basic lean bread dough, can be taken in any number of flavor directions, often with dramatic color presentations, such as with the classic spinach pasta or a tomato pasta, and can be enhanced with different fats such as olive oil, or aromatics such as pepper and thyme. This is fine, but for the most part, flavors should be added in the form of a sauce or garnish, and ingredients such as spinach are added for color more than for flavor.

### Basic Pasta Dough

The traditional method for making pasta is to form a mound of flour on your cutting board, make a cup in the center, crack the eggs into the cup, then swirl the eggs so that the flour combines gradually and evenly. But this amount of egg is somewhat difficult to contain in this amount of flour; it tends to run over the edge. So I recommend making your mound of flour in a mixing bowl and removing the dough once it has come together.

This quantity is perfect for 2 large portions or 4 appetizer portions, and because of its size is easy to mix and knead. It can, of course, be doubled. The dough should take no more than 20 minutes from start to finish. It should be allowed to rest (to relax the gluten) for at least 10 minutes after kneading and before rolling, wrapped in plastic. The dough can be refrigerated for an hour and up to 24 hours before rolling. Rolled and cut pasta can be bagged and frozen for up to a month.

*9 ounces flour (about 1½ cups)*
*6 ounces eggs (3 large eggs)*

Place the flour in a mixing bowl and make a cup in the center. Crack the eggs into the cup. Using your fingers, stir the eggs, gradually incorporating the flour. Alternately, you can combine the flour and eggs in a food processor and pulse just to mix them. When the dough comes together, remove it from the bowl or food processor bowl and knead it on a floured board or countertop, pressing it with the heel of your hand, folding it over, heel, fold, heel, fold, until it's velvety smooth. This will take 5 to 10 minutes.

Form the dough into a disk, wrap it in plastic, and let it rest for at least 10 minutes and up to 1 hour. (This dough can be refrigerated for up to 24 hours.) Cut into 4 equal pieces, roll them to the desired thinness, and cut. If you're cutting the pasta with a machine into tagliolini rather than fettuccine, it's helpful to let the sheets of pasta dry a little before you cut them or make sure they're well floured.

Another practical matter. Whatever surface you knead on will get a patina of flour and egg on it. I use the side of a large offset metal spatula to scrape this patina off the countertop, which is far quicker and easier than doing it with water and a sponge (which will just get gooey with non-water-soluble gluten)—or you can use any flat-edged metal spatula or, of course, a bench scraper, a tool made expressly for this purpose and used by bakers.

SERVES 3 TO 6

## What You Can Do Now That You Have the Pasta Dough Ratio

- Make more of it and make it often! It's beautiful just as it is. Cut into tagliolini or fettuccine and sauced simply with a flavorful olive oil and Parmigiano-Reggiano. Or served with cream and diced bacon. I prefer not to use very bold flavors, so that the flavor of the pasta can be fully appreciated, but I've also enjoyed hearty tomato sauces, such as a puttanesca, on fresh pasta.

- Because the ratio works with any quantity, and because fresh pasta freezes so well, you can make a double or triple batch to cut and freeze, to have available to put together a delicious dish at the last minute. Do not freeze the dough in a mass for later rolling; freeze cut pasta only, and add frozen pasta directly to boiling water.

- Another reason to make pasta yourself, besides the fact that it tastes like heaven and is fun to make, is that it allows you to shape the pasta as you wish. See page 148 for the French Laundry agnolotti technique, an ingenious self-sealing pasta that can be used with any soft filling, a chicken or seafood mousseline (pages 145–149), a mushroom puree, a puree of butternut squash, or even taken in a sweet direction and filled with pastry cream and served as a warm dessert, sweet agnolotti with caramel sauce.

- You can make your own lasagna very easily and with multiple layers of very thin pasta sheets—it's incomparable.

- Another excellent use of sheets is to simply cook them and spread some sort of filling on them, say a meat filling or a creamed spinach, to use some common examples, and roll them up for an instant single-portion lasagna. Slice them on a bias, top with cheese, and bake until hot. This is a great method to use for leftover braised meats and it also works well with sweet fillings.

- Pasta can be varied in the same ways bread can be; there's no reason why you couldn't make a garlic-rosemary pasta or a chipotle pasta or a lemon and black pepper pasta, but you really ought to ask yourself what you're after. Unlike flavored breads, which we eat with little adornment, pasta is usually dressed somehow, so you should have a good reason for flavoring your pasta dough, rather than adding the flavor after you've cooked it. Frankly, there are few good reasons to flavor it, unless you're marketing pasta, in which case all kinds of flavors can entice impressionable buyers.

- Color is, in fact, the most compelling reason to complicate your pasta. And of those colors, green is the most common. Green pasta (see page 20) is best made by adding blanched and shocked or sautéed spinach to basic pasta dough, with additional flour to compensate for the additional moisture. The flavor will not be especially spinachy, but the color is excellent and makes for a vivid presentation and a nutritious pasta. You might add roasted red peppers or tomato for a red pasta, and some chefs like to make black pasta with squid ink, but beyond the dramatic green or very yellow pasta made with additional yolks, colored pastas can seem gimmicky.

- The other meaningful variation on basic pasta dough, along with pasta verde, is the addition of as many egg yolks as possible for a very rich flavor and vivid yellow color (see page 21).

## Pasta Verde (Green Pasta)

Spinach pasta should be a deep rich green to add a dramatic color to an ordinary pasta dish. Because of its color, it can be sauced simply, with some cream and butter and gratings of fresh Parmigiano-Reggiano, and still give the satisfaction of a more complex dish. It will, of course, taste like fresh pasta, not fresh spinach. If you want the flavor of fresh spinach, use it on the pasta, not in it.

Thirty years ago, spinach pasta was virtually unheard of in America. When a young chef named Thomas Keller, cooking at the Palm Beach Yacht Club, wanted to try a new dish he read about in Vincent Price's *A Treasury of Great Recipes* that called for spinach pasta, he couldn't find it, and so, clever lad, he put green food coloring in the spaghetti water. The unusual color, combined with the salt leached out of the hot prosciutto, rendered the dish unappetizing and inedible. Happily, Keller would come quite a ways in the recipe department in the ensuing years.

Tellingly, the recipe for the dish is *Tagliatelle Verde con Prosciutto*—Green Pasta with Prosciutto—*green* pasta, not spinach pasta.

*3 to 4 ounces blanched, shocked spinach, squeezed of excess*
*moisture, roughly chopped (you'll need 7 to 8 ounces raw*
*spinach for 3 ounces cooked and drained)*
*12 ounces flour*
*6 ounces eggs (3 large eggs)*

Put the spinach in a food processor and pulse several times to puree it. Add the flour and eggs and process until a stiff dough comes together (if it's too moist, add more flour). Remove from the bowl and knead for 5 to

10 minutes until smooth (if it's sticky, flour your work surface liberally). Wrap and rest it for at least 10 minutes and, refrigerated, up to 24 hours. Roll and cut as desired.

YIELD: 20 OUNCES PASTA DOUGH, 4 TO 6 PORTIONS

## Rich Egg Yolk Pasta

This very rich, flavorful (and sticky) dough is delicious as is, just dressed with a little olive oil and Parmigiano-Reggiano, but it also makes wonderful ravioli.

*10 ounces flour*
*6 ounces egg yolks (7 to 10 yolks or ½ to ⅔ cup)*
*2 ounces egg (1 large egg)*
*1 ounce water*
*½ ounce olive oil*

Put the flour in a mixing bowl and stir a small hole in the center of the flour. Put the remaining ingredients in the hole and stir the yolks and liquid with your fingers to gradually incorporate the flour into the yolks. When the dough has formed, remove it from the bowl and knead it just until it comes together. Shape it into a rectangle and wrap and rest it for at least 10 minutes and, refrigerated, up to 24 hours. Roll and cut as desired.

YIELD: 18 OUNCES PASTA DOUGH, 4 PORTIONS

# Pie Dough

## Pie Dough = 3 parts flour : 2 parts fat : 1 part water

The 3-2-1 pie dough is one of my favorite ratios because it allows me to make a pie or tart dough without even thinking, and so it makes me feel like I know what I'm doing in the pastry kitchen, even if I don't. It's so standard and useful that in my CIA textbook, it's called 3-2-1 Pie Dough—the ratio is its name. There are all kinds of doughs you can make, with different fats, different flours, ground nuts, sugars, aromatics, but the 3-2-1 pie dough can't be beat.

I like to use whole butter as the fat, which results in a rich flavorful dough. Lard is another excellent choice, especially for savory preparations. Vegetable shortening is the most neutral tasting of the fats available (be sure your hydrogenated vegetable doesn't contain trans fats, which have been linked to the same health problems as saturated meat fats). The ingredients here are measured by weight rather than by volume, a decided boon you'll find when measuring shortening.

I made the following ratio simply because 2 sticks of butter, 8 ounces, was convenient and 12 ounces of flour

*A flaky piecrust is achieved by creating multiple ▶ layers of dough separated by butter, lard, or shortening. The other important factor in a piecrust is tenderness—crusts will be dense and tough if you overwork the dough. When you add the liquid to the flour and fat, mix the dough gently and just until it comes together, then wrap it in plastic and refrigerate it for at least 15 minutes or until you're ready to roll it.*

seemed like the right amount for a pie; please note that because butter contains 15 percent water and 80 percent butterfat, 6.4 ounces fat and 1.2 ounces water, this is not a strict adherence to the ratio and the amount of water you need can vary; the flavor of the fat makes up for the missing 20 percent, but you can make this dough with shortening or butter. The 12 ounces of flour, about 2¼ cups, is enough for one 9-inch pie pan with enough left over to fashion a solid or a lattice cover or one quiche shell, or half can be refrigerated for a day or frozen for another use. Half this recipe will be enough for a 9-inch tart pan.

Variations follow a few threads: savory, sweet, and nut. The above dough is also known as *pâte brisée,* which refers to a straightforward pastry dough (*brisée* means "broken" and refers to the crumbly nature of the dough as opposed to an elastic dough or a dough containing egg). Its counterpart is the *pâte sucrée,* which includes sugar, for sweet doughs. To push the dough definitively into savory, ¼ cup or so of grated Parmigiano-Reggiano can be added to the dough. Also, pulverized nuts such as pine nuts or almonds, toasted or raw, can replace some of the flour for a more flavorful dough.

As far as technique goes, pie dough can be mixed by hand, in a food processor, or in a standing mixer. Because it's so easy to do by hand, and faster, that's what I prefer—it saves time washing appliance bowls and blades. When mixing by hand, it's important that the fat is very cold, that you work quickly, and that you work the dough as little as possible (don't squeeze it or knead it, just press it gently together). If using a food processor, you can freeze your fat for the best results. Regardless of your choice of method, the rationale behind the steps remains the same: flour and fat are combined or "rubbed," then enough water is added just to bring them together into a dough. When you combine the flour and fat, you want to create small beads of fat and plenty of pea-sized chunks for a flaky crust (the fat separates the layers of flour and water); the colder the fat, the better. Overmixing or kneading it will result in the development of too much gluten (as will adding too much water) and thus a tough dough. Keep the fat cool by using ice water. When the dough just comes together, it's wrapped in plastic and refrigerated for 15 minutes or until you're ready to roll it. And that's all there is to it. It takes 10 minutes given a scale and a bowl.

## 3-2-1 Pie Dough (Pâte Brisée)

*12 ounces flour*
*8 ounces butter (2 sticks; or lard or shortening or any combination*
*    thereof), cut into small pieces, cold or even frozen*
*2 to 4 ounces ice water (quantity depends on the fat—whole*
*    butter has water in it, so you only need a couple of ounces;*
*    shortening and lard do not)*
*3-fingered pinch of salt (about ½ teaspoon)*

Combine the flour and butter in a mixing bowl and rub the butter between your fingers until you have small beads of fat and plenty of pea-sized chunks. If you're making a bigger batch, this can be done in a standing mixer with a paddle attachment, but remember not to paddle too much after you add the water, just enough so that it comes together. Add the ice water gradually and a good pinch of salt and mix gently, just until combined; if you work the dough too hard, it will become tough. Shape the dough into 2 equal disks and refrigerate for 15 minutes or until ready to roll.

YIELD: I PIE SHELL AND LID OR TWO 9-INCH TART CRUSTS

The dough can be used raw with other ingredients as with an apple pie. But often you'll need to bake the shell first, as for a quiche or when cooking a liquid batter. This is called blind baking.

To blind bake a crust, you need to fill the shell with something heavy to prevent the crust from buckling. Pie weights are made specifically for this, but a layer of aluminum foil and a pound of dried beans reserved for just this purpose does the job well. Preheat your oven to 325°F. Line the pie dough with parchment or foil and weight the bottom of your shell with pie weights or beans and bake for 20 to 25 minutes. Remove the weights or beans and continue baking until the crust is golden brown and cooked through, another 15 minutes or so.

## What You Can Do Now That You Have the 3-2-1 Pie Dough Ratio

What I like best about this ratio is that it takes pies and tarts from being open-a-book, plan-in-advance items into the realm of spontaneity. Savory and sweet tarts can often be made simply with what's on hand, say some onions and cheese. The discovery of fresh peaches or rhubarb at a farmers' market can, on a whim, result in a pie later in the day. Pie shells and tart shells are vehicles for other ingredients. When you think of this dough as a vehicle, whole worlds open up to you.

### VARIATIONS ON THE DOUGH

- For sweet pies and tarts, make *pâte sucrée*—add 2 tablespoons of sugar to the 3-2-1 pie dough recipe, or about 1 tablespoon per cup of flour.
- The 3-2-1 pie dough can be used as a shell or crust for any pie or tart; no sugar is added to *pâte brisée,* though other savory elements may be, such as ¼ cup freshly grated Parmigiano-Reggiano to the above 3-2-1 pie dough.
- You can make this dough extra flaky by treating it like a puff pastry dough, which is composed of hundreds of layers created by successive folding and rolling out of the dough to increase the layers exponentially. Leave the butter in larger chunks when mixing. Shape the dough into a rectangle about ½ inch thick, wrap and refrigerate it for an hour or more, remove from the refrigerator, and let it temper; that is, let the butter soften a little so that it becomes pliable. Fold the rectangle in thirds and roll out into a rectangle about ½ inch thick, wrap, and refrigerate. Repeat this one more time (or up to three more times if you wish). This is an excellent technique for rustic free-form fruit tarts. (This is also a method for making wonderfully flaky biscuits, page 34).
- For a nut crust, which is especially good with fruit and citrus tarts, pulverize 1 cup of nuts—such as almonds, pecans, pine nuts, wal-

nuts, cashews, pistachios—and combine it with the flour in half the 3-2-1 pie dough as well as 1 egg and a teaspoon of vanilla.

- For savory meat pies, use 2 parts rendered pork fat, called lard. This makes a good empanada dough as well for individual fried pies filled with shredded pork shoulder or any braised meat.
- *Individual tarts.* Ramekins and other small ovenproof pans can be used to make individual tarts.
- *Free-form tart.* This dough can be shaped by hand into a free-form tart. One of the easiest free-form tarts is to roll out your dough to the desired size, place it on a baking sheet, and spread out your ingredients on it, leaving a 1-inch border that can be rolled or pinched up to form the edge. If you have a peel and a baking stone, you can form the tart right on the peel, dusted with cornmeal or semolina, and slide the tart onto a baking stone in a preheated oven.

## Tart Variations

The tart is a vehicle for any flavor or delicious ingredient you want it to carry. Most of the following can be prepared in a tart shell or a pie shell, though a tart is more elegant and a pie shell will change the depth, and therefore the nature, of the dish. And if you want to go rustic, use a free-form shape. Nine ounces of flour and 1½ sticks of butter (6 ounces) and 2 to 3 ounces of water will give you the right amount for one 9-inch tart shell. If you're filling it with a custard, you'll need between 1 and 2 cups of custard, depending how loaded your tart is with garnish.

- *Caramelized onion and Comté tart.* Deeply caramelize 4 Spanish onions; let cool. Top a baked 9-inch tart shell with grated Comté cheese (or Emmental) and spread the onions evenly over the cheese. Bake in a 350°F oven until the cheese and onions are hot.
- *Sautéed leek and walnut tart.* Clean and thinly slice 3 leeks, white and light green parts only. Sauté them in butter over medium heat with salt and pepper until they're tender. Add a couple of teaspoons of Dijon or a teaspoon of sherry vinegar if you wish. Make

a standard custard (see ratio, page 199) by mixing 1 cup of half-and-half and 2 large eggs, ½ teaspoon salt, and several grinds of pepper. Spread the leeks over a prebaked tart shell, sprinkle a layer of chopped toasted walnuts over the leeks, pour in the custard, sprinkle with grated Gruyère cheese, and bake at 325°F until set, about 30 minutes. You can substitute sautéed spinach or sautéed mushrooms for the leeks.

- *Potato and leek tart.* Prepare 4 leeks as above. Blind bake a 3-2-1 pie dough in a pie plate or cake pan (the latter lined with parchment). Spread a layer of thinly sliced peeled potatoes on the bottom of the crust. Spread a layer of thinly sliced leeks over the potatoes. Repeat this for 2 layers of leeks and sprinkle liberally with salt, pepper, Parmigiano-Reggiano, and some gratings of nutmeg. Add enough cream to just cover the potatoes. Top with ¼ cup Comté or Emmental. Bake at 400°F until the potatoes are tender and the cream has reduced and thickened, about 45 minutes to 1 hour.

- *Tomato tart.* When tomatoes are in season, abundant, and colorful (Early Girl, Green Zebra), spread a layer of slices in a free-form tart shell, sprinkle with salt, pepper, thyme leaves, and drizzle or mist with olive oil. Bake in a medium-hot oven until the tomatoes are hot and their liquid has reduced.

- *Peach and prosciutto tart.* Layer a tart shell with prosciutto; layer thin slices of peaches on top of the prosciutto and bake until the crust is done and the peaches are dense and cooked through. Garnish with torn or chiffonaded arugula.

- *Chocolate-vanilla tart.* Spread a layer of pastry cream (page 215) on the bottom of a baked tart shell. Make 8 ounces of ganache (page 221) and when it has cooled but is pourable, top the pastry cream with it. Chill thoroughly. Garnish with whipped cream or powdered sugar.

- *Caramel-chocolate tart.* Pour a layer of caramel sauce (page 223) on the bottom of a baked tart shell and cover with ganache (page 221) as in the tart above.

- *Lemon tart.* For a quick lemon curd, combine ½ cup lemon juice, ½ cup sugar, and 4 egg yolks in a large microwave-safe mixing bowl and whisk thoroughly to combine. Microwave on high in 30-second intervals, whisking after each interval until the mixture is thick and custardy, about 4 minutes total. Whisk in 2 ounces of butter. Pour the lemon curd into a baked 9-inch tart shell and chill. Lightly brown the tart beneath a broiler and garnish with powdered sugar.

- *Berry tart.* Fill a baked pie shell with pastry cream (page 215) and garnish with concentric rings of blueberries, raspberries, strawberries, and blackberries.
- *Blueberry-custard tart.* Spread a handful or two of blueberries in a baked tart shell; if there are any cracks in the tart shell, patch them with raw dough. Combine the ingredients for crème brûlée (page 214) using 1½ cups of half-and-half, 3 eggs, and ⅓ cup of sugar, and pour over the berries. Bake in a 300°F oven until the custard is set, 20 to 30 minutes.
- *Any-fruit fruit tart.* Apple, peach, rhubarb, blackberry, plum, apricot, and other such fruits can be used with a free-form shell for a quick and easy sweet tart. The only variation is the amount of sugar added—a few tablespoons for apple and stone fruits, more for tart fruits such as rhubarb and blackberry. Rhubarb and blackberry and fruits that bake very wet benefit from a tablespoon of cornstarch per cup of fruit, though without a crust on top, much of the liquid will cook off.

## PIES

Fruit pies are a great pleasure of the summer in our house, with a thriving farmers' market nearby selling rhubarb in spring, apples and pumpkin in fall. There are endless fruit pie recipes out there, but there's no reason you can't improvise on what you already know, and season by eye, remembering that tart fruits require a good deal more sugar than pies made with naturally sweet fruits.

But pies shouldn't be relegated to the sweet. One of the best pies there is, and an easy one and an economical one, is the chicken pot pie (or beef, fish, or vegetable). Line 8-ounce ramekins or other individual, ovenproof dishes with the 3-2-1 pie dough. Make a thick cream soup (see page 115), adding a new main ingredient, such as cooked chicken or beef, along with onions, carrots, and celery. Top with a crust, make holes for steam to escape, and bake at 350°F for 45 minutes or so, until the crust is done. This is a great dish to make with leftover roast chicken and a stock from the carcass.

A free-form pie dough can also be shaped to hold a *pâté* mixture (a *farce,* or forcemeat)—in other words, a more thoroughly mixed meat loaf (see page 140). When these are done in a terrine mold, they are called *pâté en croute,* and when they are free form, they become the English meat pie. These can be eaten hot or cold. When eaten cold, aspic is poured through a central steam hole to fill space between the crust and the meat, which can shrink during cooking.

### *Addison's Bebop-a-Rebop Rhubarb Pie with Lattice Crust*

My favorite pie, the one that heralds the arrival of spring as much as fresh peas and lettuces, is rhubarb pie. Nothing beats this vegetable for its tartness, its green and red color intrigues, and the fact that its leaves are poisonous adds mystery and danger to the notion of it (though, of course, there is no actual danger). My daughter has always loved this pie, since her little girl days when she delighted in Garrison Keillor's alliterative ditty by which we call this pie, and which we season with cinnamon and cloves. I love a buttery flaky crust, but because rhubarb releases so much liquid during cooking, it needs plenty of reduction, making a very open crust, a lattice crust, desirable.

For the crust, make a 3-2-1 pie dough (page 24), using 15 ounces flour (about 3 cups), 10 ounces butter, and 5 ounces ice water.

> *12 ounces sugar (1½ cups)*
> *1½ teaspoons ground cinnamon*
> *¼ teaspoon ground cloves*
> *⅛ cup cornstarch*
> *1½ pounds rhubarb, small diced (about 5 cups)*

Preheat your oven to 425°F.

Roll out your dough into a large rectangle about ³⁄₁₆ inch thick. Invert your pie plate on the dough and use the rest for strips. It needs to be large enough to fill a pie plate and for nine ¾-inch-wide strips the diameter of the pie plate. You may also cut one-third of the dough off and roll out separately for strips.

Lay the dough into the pie plate, leaving about an inch of dough overhanging the edge. Using a pastry wheel or knife, cut the remaining dough into nine ¾-inch-wide strips the length of the pie plate (not all need to be that long, but at least five do).

Combine the sugar, spices, and cornstarch and stir to distribute the spices and cornstarch. In a large bowl, toss the rhubarb with the sugar mixture until it's evenly coated. Pour the rhubarb and sugar into the pie plate. Place 5 strips of dough horizontally at even intervals across the pie. Fold the first, third, and fifth strips back to the edge and lay one strip of dough vertically across the horizontal strips. Fold the first, third, and fifth horizontal strips back, then fold the second and fourth strips back to the first verticle strip. Lay a second verticle strip an equal distance from the first one. Fold the second and fourth strips back. Repeat the process with the final lattice strips. Fold the overhanging dough over the lattice edges and crimp the dough along the circumference of the pie dish.

Place the pie on a baking sheet and bake for 1 to 1¼ hours, until the fruit is bubbling and hot and the crust is golden brown. Allow to cool completely before cutting.

YIELD: ONE 9-INCH PIE

# Biscuit Dough

## Biscuit = 3 parts flour : 1 part fat : 2 parts liquid

Flaky, buttery biscuits are no more difficult to make than pie dough and they use the exact same ingredients with one important difference: the amount of fat and liquid are reversed—they use twice as much liquid as fat. This results in more gluten, and therefore more doughiness, more chewiness, rather than a more crumbly, tender crust. Instead of being a 3-2-1 dough—flour, fat, liquid—biscuits use a 3 : 1 : 2 ratio, 3 parts flour, 1 part fat, 2 parts liquid. The ratio should be easy to remember for those in the Chicago area code, so I call these Chicago biscuits.

I also include salt for flavor—this is kind of a cross between bread dough and pie dough, and the simple nature of the ingredients requires it. You can achieve leavening through a folding and rolling of the dough alone, but I like to include some baking powder, about a teaspoon per 4 ounces of flour (a scant cup).

Otherwise, the same rules apply for biscuits as for pie dough. Cold diced butter is cut or rubbed into the flour; the liquid (in this case, milk) is mixed in just until the dough comes together. (For drop biscuits, more milk is added and the dough is spooned directly onto a baking sheet.) The dough is then shaped into a rectangle and chilled to solidify the butter and allow the gluten to relax.

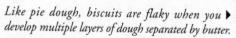

*Like pie dough, biscuits are flaky when you* ▶
*develop multiple layers of dough separated by butter.*

What creates flakiness in pastries and doughs are multiple layers of butter between the dough, the same as in puff pastry and flaky pie dough: water in the butter vaporizes in the heat and air expands, separating the layers of dough. To make puff pastry, the layer of butter is highly controlled. A chunk of butter is enclosed in dough and rolled out to make 1 relatively thick layer of butter between 2 sheets of dough; the dough is then folded in thirds, like a letter, and rolled out again, creating 3 layers of butter between 4 layers of dough. The dough is chilled and folded again in thirds to create 9 layers of butter between 10 layers of dough. Chill, fold, roll again (each of these is called a "turn"): 27 layers of butter between 28 layers of dough. Again: 81 layers of butter, 82 layers of dough. Again: 243 layers of butter, 244 layers of dough. And a final "turn," 6 in all: 729 layers of butter between 730 layers of dough. When this dough is rolled out to ¼ inch, then baked, those hundreds of layers puff and separate, creating an exquisitely flaky delicate tender pastry, puff pastry. Or as Harold McGee puts it in *On Food and Cooking,* each layer of dough is microscopically thin, thinner than paper, thin as an individual starch granule, and when baked, these very thin layers "shatter in the mouth into small delicate shards."

When making flaky rolled biscuits (or a flaky piecrust), the same principle is used, but the layers of butter are not uniform, they're irregular, slanted, of varying lengths and thicknesses, creating irregular sheets of fat between sheets of dough. The rolling of the dough develops the gluten and so these sheets become elastic and chewy rather than crumbly (as with the pie dough) to create the uniquely crisp-on-the-outside, soft-and-buttery-on-the-inside biscuit. It's a marvel.

### Chicago Biscuits (3-1-2 Biscuits)

Biscuits are one of those great preparations that support with equal grace a sweet sauce or a savory one, strawberries and whipped cream or a spicy sausage gravy, perfect for breakfast and excellent for dinner. The butter is prominent in these biscuits, so use good butter. Traditionally, these are cut into rounds, but at home you may simply want to cut them into squares to avoid wasting the trim. Use a sharp knife to keep the layers on the edges distinct.

*9 ounces flour (a scant 2 cups)*
*2 teaspoons baking powder*
*1 teaspoon salt*
*3 ounces chilled butter, diced*
*6 ounces milk*

Set a mixing bowl on a scale and pour in the flour. Add the baking powder (pressed through a strainer if it's pebbly) and salt. Weigh out the butter. Rub and pinch the butter into the flour so that the butter is well distributed and in fragments and small chunks, the largest of which are not bigger than peas. Pour in the milk and combine just until a dough is formed (you will see distinct whole chunks of butter in the dough). Form into a 4- by 6-inch rectangle, wrap in plastic, and refrigerate for at least an hour.

Unwrap the dough and dust it with flour. Roll the dough out to about three times its size on a floured countertop, board, or plastic wrap, maintaining the rectangular shape. Fold it into thirds and roll it out again (it will be more resistant and springy now). Fold it in thirds again, press it down firmly, wrap it in plastic wrap, and refrigerate for at least an hour or until thoroughly chilled. Repeat the procedure again. The dough is now ready to be rolled out to ½ inch thick and cut, or it can be folded in thirds, refrigerated, and rolled out again one more time for a total of 6 folds or turns.

Cut the dough into squares or, if you like, into rounds with a ring cutter or a thin glass. Bake at 400°F until done, 20 to 30 minutes.

YIELD: 4 TO 6 BISCUITS

# Cookie Dough

## Cookie Dough = 1 part sugar : 2 parts fat : 3 parts flour

This is chef and teacher Bob del Grosso's favorite example of a kitchen ratio, and his affection for it is instructive about ratios generally. Bob is a friend and adviser and this recipe, as he has noted, will not give you art or the best cookie ever made. But it will give you a good solid short cookie and, in so doing, instruct the thoughtful cook about proportions in a short sweet dough and the nature of a cookie. One part sugar, 2 parts fat, 3 parts flour, will result in a cookie with the right texture and crunch, and the right balance of fat and sugar. It is, of course, very plain—sugar, butter, and flour—a shortbread. I appreciate most its level of sweetness—just enough to satisfy, but not so much that it's cloying. The quality of the butter, the only ingredient with significant flavor, is important. Don't use butter that's been sitting around for a while; use good flavorful butter. I use either salted or unsalted—I think these cookies benefit from a little salt, so if you prefer unsalted butter (and when you bake, this does give you a little more control), consider adding a pinch of salt. But use good butter and fresh flour. In this plainness is its excellence. And, of course, the dough is easily enhanced in any number of ways, depending on additional ingredients (nuts, candy,

*These lemon–poppy seed cookies use a standard* ▶
*cookie ratio of 3 parts flour, 2 parts fat, and 1 part sugar.*

seeds), flavors (extracts, zests), or garnish (sprinkles, colored sugars, flavored glazes).

So, unlike any of the other dough ratios, all of which are typically enjoyed as they are and without adornment, you would almost never simply use the cookie dough recipe as is, but would typically add some kind of additional ingredients.

It's a good recipe to do once though, without anything extraneous, so that you can understand what a cookie is. Taste a plain cookie, note its texture, note the level of sweetness, the flavor of the butter, the flavor contributed by the flour. And because it's a solid ratio, you can make a small quantity quickly—an ounce of sugar, creamed into ½ stick of butter, with 3 ounces of flour folded in. This will result in what can be considered the essence of a cookie. Take any single ingredient away and it ceases to be a cookie, becomes something else entirely; take away the sugar and you have roux or *beurre manié*, take away the flour and you have icing. This ratio is a diamond.

But simply add a topping of chopped almonds or pistachios and it becomes a superb cookie. Some friends who helped me test these recipes referred to them as adult cookies. My kids will sneak these cookies, so they're not only for adults, but I do understand the comment. They're not chewy and rich with fat. If you're looking for something light to offer after dinner with coffee, or with afternoon tea, or a midmorning snack to munch on, these are a pleasure.

### 1-2-3 Cookie Dough: The Essence-of-a-Cookie Cookie

*2 ounces sugar (about 4½ tablespoons)*
*4 ounces unsalted butter (1 stick), soft but not melted*
*6 ounces flour (1 to 1¼ cups)*

Combine the sugar and butter, and mix, beat, or whisk until the sugar is evenly distributed and the butter has become light in color. (It wouldn't hurt if you added a pinch of salt and ½ teaspoon of vanilla here.) Fold in the flour gradually and continue to mix until a uniform dough is formed. I prefer these cookies very thin and so roll them into a log using plastic wrap, chill them, and slice them about ⅜ inch thick. Or you can roll the dough into 1½-inch balls, place them on a baking sheet, and press them down to a thickness of ¼ inch or as desired. Bake in a 350°F oven until cooked through, 15 to 20 minutes. Because there is relatively little fat, these cookies will not spread out as they bake. This recipe will give you 5 to 10 cookies.

## What You Can Do Now That You Have the 1-2-3 Cookie Dough Ratio

What I like best is that I can make cookies at the last minute, as many or as little as I need or would like. Five minutes, and they're in the oven. But also, the recipe teaches you about how these fundamental ingredients, flour, sugar, and butter, interact. Variations are infinite and fall into three categories—changing the flavor, swapping an ingredient, or altering the proportion of flour relative to the fat and sugar.

- The flavor variations are what make the plain cookie distinctive. Some simple variations that add flavor, crunch, and visual appeal to these are nuts. Shape the dough into balls, press the balls into chopped almonds before placing them on the baking sheet, and press them to the desired thickness.
- Other nuts that are excellent to use with these cookies: chopped or whole pistachios (for the most visual appeal, use blanched and peeled pistachios), walnuts, hazelnuts, macadamia nuts, and cashews. For color and flavor, pistachios are my favorite.
- A final nut variation is to pulverize the nuts and replace ⅓ the flour with your nut powder. This is a version of Linzer dough, which has hazelnuts.
- Add a teaspoon of poppy seeds, the grated zest of 1 lemon, and ¼ teaspoon of vanilla to the above essence-of-a-cookie recipe for Lemon–Poppy Seed Cookies (page 41).
- Add ¼ teaspoon each of cinnamon, cloves, and nutmeg.
- Add ½ teaspoon of almond extract.
- Add chocolate. Melt 3 ounces of good semisweet or bittersweet chocolate, sift the flour over it, and fold it into the butter and sugar. (This could be in other categories of variations—in the

sugar category because it sweetens, and in the fat category, because it adds fat.)

- Instead of chocolate, add peanut butter.

Another ingredient you can vary is the type of sugar used.

- Use brown sugar instead of white sugar for a darker cookie with a more complex sweetness that is a little chewier and quicker to brown.
- Use agave nectar for a cookie with a lower glycemic index. (The glycemic index describes the speed with which carbohydrates break down and release glucose in the body; foods with a low glycemic index have been shown to have beneficial effects on the body.) Used at the same ratio as sugar, this will result in a sweeter cookie than one using white sugar.
- Use a combination of sugar and molasses (see the spice cookies on page 42 for a variation).
- Use a combination of sugar and honey.

The last ingredient to alternate is the butter. Try using different saturated fats (fats that are solid at room temperature).

- When making flavored cookies, you can use a vegetable shortening, which gives the cookies a distinct crispness. Lard can replace the butter as well, but, again, do this only when you're adding a lot of other flavors to the dough because the lard can add a distinctive savory, even porky, note to the cookie. You may want to add a teaspoon or so of water or milk when using a rendered fat, which has no water (butter contains about 15 percent water).
- Use other pliable animal fats to create a cookie to accompany a savory dish.

Other issues:

- Adding other ingredients such as eggs and baking powder change the nature of the cookie as well. Both will help give a little softer, airier crumb. Adding whipped egg whites results in a different kind of cookie, a delicate tuile. A common tuile ratio is equal parts egg white, sugar, and flour; stir in another part melted butter and some almond extract for French almond tuile.

- Varying the ratio will give you a different quality cookie. If you make a cookie dough of equal parts sugar, butter, and flour, you'll get a very rich chewy cookie—often called drop cookies because they're dropped from a spoon onto the baking sheet—but a little on the oily side without the addition of other ingredients such as eggs and some sort of garnish, such as chocolate chips. Some recipes reduce the butter to one-half the amount. Increasing the ratio of sugar will give you a crisper cookie.

## Classic Variations We Know by Other Names

### Lemon–Poppy Seed Cookies

The lemon–poppy seed combination is one of my favorites, in both cakes and cookies. I love the fresh flavor the citrus zest brings. I have no idea what the poppy seeds, which are 50 percent fat by weight, bring, except to say that it's a completely different, and lesser, cookie if you leave them out.

> *6 ounces sugar (about ⅔ cup)*
> *12 ounces butter (3 sticks), soft but not melted*
> *1 large egg (optional)*
> *1 tablespoon poppy seeds*
> *Zest of 3 lemons*
> *1 teaspoon vanilla extract*
> *18 ounces flour*

Preheat your oven to 350°F.

Combine the sugar and butter in a standing mixer with the paddle attachment, and mix on medium speed, scraping the butter down as necessary, until the sugar is evenly distributed and the butter has become light in color. Add the egg, if using, while mixing until incorporated, then add the poppy seeds, zest, and vanilla. Add the flour gradually and continue to mix until a uniform dough comes together. Roll into 1-inch balls, place them on a baking sheet, press down to a thickness of between ¼ and ½ inch or as desired, and bake until cooked through. This dough can also be shaped into a log using plastic wrap or parchment paper, chilled, and sliced.

YIELD: ABOUT 30 COOKIES

## Rip's Spice Cookies

This was my father's favorite cookie, a variant of the ginger cookie, and I've adapted it here as a contrast to the 1-2-3 cookie: it uses nearly a 1 to 1 ratio of fat to flour, plus 1 egg, and so has a good deal more give in its bite and more richness in feel than the drier, shortbreadlike 3-2-1 cookie.

Using a scale to measure the shortening makes for much cleaner work than measuring shortening by volume. This recipe calls for 10 ounces (about 1½ cups by volume) of shortening. Place your mixing bowl on a scale, zero it, and add 10 ounces of the shortening.

Pay attention here to a shift in the ratio: this recipe calls for a nearly equal ratio of flour, fat, and sugar. Because of this, the cookies will spread out, so leave some room between cookies on the baking sheet. The egg and baking powder will give the cookie a little lift, a slightly less dense crumb.

*10 ounces vegetable shortening (1½ cups)*
*8 ounces sugar (about 1 cup)*
*1 large egg*
*¼ cup molasses*
*12 ounces flour (about 2 cups)*
*1 teaspoon baking powder*
*2 teaspoons ground cinnamon*
*1 teaspoon ground ginger*
*¼ teaspoon salt*

Preheat your oven to 350°F.

Combine the shortening, sugar, and egg and mix thoroughly in a standing mixer or by hand. Add the molasses and continue mixing. Combine the remaining ingredients and fold them into the dough.

Roll into small balls or spoon out tablespoons of dough onto a baking sheet. Give them some room because they'll spread. Bake for 15 minutes or until the edges begin to darken.

YIELD: ABOUT 24 COOKIES

## Classic Chocolate Chip Cookies

This recipe calls for equal parts butter, sugar, and flour, so has a very high proportion of fat, which will cause them to spread considerably and result in a very thin crisp chocolate chip cookie. If you prefer your cookies crisper, reduce the butter to 4 ounces.

*8 ounces unsalted butter (2 sticks)*
*4 ounces white sugar (about ½ cup)*
*4 ounces brown sugar (about ½ cup)*
*1 large egg*
*1 teaspoon vanilla extract*
*½ teaspoon salt*
*8 ounces flour (about 1¾ cups)*
*1 teaspoon baking powder*
*1 cup chocolate chips or chopped chocolate*

Preheat your oven to 350°F.

Combine the butter, sugars, egg, and vanilla and mix thoroughly in a standing mixer using the paddle attachment or by hand. Combine the remaining ingredients except the chocolate and fold them into the dough. Fold the chocolate into the dough.

Drop heaping tablespoons onto a baking sheet. Give them some room because they'll spread. Bake for 10 minutes or until the edges begin to darken.

YIELD: ABOUT 24 COOKIES

## Classic Sugar Cookies

A similar variation to the chocolate chip cookie—but here, equal parts butter and sugar are combined with egg and 50 percent more flour, or 1.5 parts flour. Also, only white sugar is used. These can be sprinkled with colored sugar, coarse sugar, or coarsely chopped almonds for visual appeal.

> 8 ounces unsalted butter (2 sticks)
> 8 ounces sugar (about 1 cup)
> 1 large egg
> 1 teaspoon vanilla extract
> ½ teaspoon salt
> 12 ounces flour (about 2 cups)
> 1 teaspoon baking powder
> Optional garnish: colored sugar, coarse sugar, or coarsely
>    chopped almonds

Preheat your oven to 350°F.

Combine the butter, sugar, egg, and vanilla and mix thoroughly in a standing mixer or by hand. Combine the remaining ingredients, except garnish, and fold them into the dough. Wrap the dough in plastic wrap and refrigerate until thoroughly chilled.

This dough can be rolled out flat and the cookies can be cut out from it. It can be shaped into individual balls and flattened with the bottom of a glass. It can be rolled into a cylinder, chilled, and sliced. Sprinkle with garnish, if desired.

Bake for 15 minutes or until done (slightly brown around edges).

**YIELD: ABOUT 24 COOKIES**

# Pâte à Choux

**Pâte à Choux = 2 parts water : 1 part butter : 1 part flour : 2 parts egg**

*P*âte à choux is one of the coolest flour-and-water preparations in the kitchen. It is easy to make, delicious all by itself, can be a pedestal for any number of sweet or savory ingredients, can be cooked in the oven, in water, in oil (with each type of heat creating different and wonderful effects), and can be featured at virtually any part of the meal. In spite of these features, it's not typically a part of the home cook's repertoire. Why? I have no idea, but I hope it changes.

*Pâte à choux,* also known as choux paste or cream puff dough, defies a precise label. It's not really a dough and it's not really a batter, though it goes through the stages of both. It begins as a loose combination of water, butter, and flour, more water than flour, like a batter. But this batter is quickly cooked, the flour absorbs the water, the starch gelatinizes, and the mixture becomes stiff, more doughlike. Then eggs are added, beaten into the dough, and the dough thins out, heading back in the direction of a batter. What you have then is a partially cooked dough batter that, when baked, puffs into an airy delicate bread that can be filled (often with cream for cream puffs) or coated (often with melted chocolate, as with a chocolate

*When choux paste is baked, vaporizing water ▶ causes the dough to puff and creates an airy crumb, as in this gougère. The crumb also allows such preparations as this or the sweet profiterole to be stuffed with a savory or sweet filling.*

◀ *The* mise en place *for* pâte à choux, *an ingenious preparation that's underused in the home kitchen even though it is easy, economical, and versatile and results in such choux-based wonders as cheese puffs, profiteroles, gnocchi, and doughnuts.*

éclair). A different take on the cream puff/éclair is the profiterole, which sandwiches ice cream and gets a dose of chocolate sauce on top. In the classic bistro dessert the Paris-Brest, it's piped into the shape of a tire, layered with cream, and garnished with almonds.

*Pâte à choux* is often flavored with cheese for a savory treat (gougère). It can be piped out of a bag into simmering water, a preparation called parisienne gnocchi, and used like pasta. Or it can be piped out of a bag into hot oil, then sprinkled with sugar, like beignets in France, delicious little doughnuts, called, in a bit of choice French naming, *pets de nonne,* or nun's farts. It's the dough used for churros in Mexico, flavored with cinnamon sugar, and the American variant, funnel cake. It's sometimes used as a panade for *pâtés* for binding and texture (try it in your meat loaf!). It's also used to bind mashed potatoes, which are then piped out and deep-fried, a preparation called pommes dauphine (the choux paste leavens the croquettes); alternately, you can mix it with leftover mashed potatoes—⅔ potato, ⅓ *pâte à choux*—form disks, flour them, and panfry for exquisitely light potato pancakes. Milk or a flavored liquid (such as stock) can be used in place of water. Or it can even, with some tweaking, be treated almost like a polenta by using semolina flour, spread on a sheet tray, cooled, and cut into shapes to be grilled or sautéed (a preparation called Gnocchi à la Romaine, page 51). There's no end to what you can do with this stuff.

## *Basic* Pâte à Choux

This is the base for just about all *pâte à choux* preparations—2 parts water, 1 part butter, 1 part flour, and 2 parts egg (plus salt for flavor). For those not using a scale, this alternate ratio by volume also works: *Pâte à choux* by volume = 1 cup water : ½ cup butter : 1 cup flour : 1 cup egg.

Choux paste can be made start to finish using a saucepan and a sturdy wooden spoon if that's your desire or if you don't have a standing mixer, beating in the eggs by hand, but I've found that you get a better puff or rise when you beat the eggs in with a mixer. An electric beater will also work with this preparation. Either way, the water takes longer to boil than it does for you to actually make the choux paste, so there's no excuse for not making *pâte à choux* preparations at home. The 1-cup ratio results in about 4 portions of gnocchi, or about 8 portions of puffs served before or after a meal as gougères or cream puffs or profiteroles.

> *8 ounces water*
> *4 ounces butter (1 stick)*
> *½ teaspoon salt*
> *4 ounces flour (a scant cup)*
> *8 ounces eggs (4 large eggs)*

Bring the water, butter, and salt to a simmer over high heat. Reduce the heat to medium, add the flour, and stir rapidly. The flour will absorb the water quickly and a dough will form and pull away from the sides. Keep stirring to continue cooking the flour and cook off some of the water, another minute or two. Remove your pan from the heat and let it cool slightly, a few minutes, or cool off the pan itself by running cold water over its base. You don't want to cook the eggs too quickly, but the choux paste needs to be warm to hot. Add the eggs one at a time, stirring rapidly until each is combined into the paste; it takes a few seconds—at first it will seem as though the dough won't accept them. The paste will go from shiny to flat, slippery to furry, when the eggs are fully in. Alternately, transfer the butter-flour paste to the bowl of a standing mixer fitted with the paddle and mix in the eggs one at a time.

The *pâté a choux* can be cooked immediately or refrigerated for up to a day until ready to use.

YIELD: ABOUT 20 OUNCES OR 24 GOUGÈRES OR PROFITEROLES

## Gougères

To the basic *pâte à choux* ingredients, add an additional teaspoon of salt to the water, and stir in ½ cup of grated Parmigiano-Reggiano or Gruyère after the eggs have been incorporated. Comté or Emmental is often used for gougères, but I love the Reggiano.

On a parchment- or Silpat-lined baking sheet, pipe or spoon out golf-ball-sized portions. Wet your finger with water or milk and press down any peaks, which can burn. Place the gougères in an oven preheated to 425°F. Reduce the heat to 350°F after 10 minutes to complete their cooking, 10 to 20 minutes longer. Taste or cut into one to judge the doneness.

*Gougère canapé variation.* Add freshly ground black pepper, crushed fennel seed, or chopped sage, rosemary, or other sturdy herbs to the *pâte à choux* dough. Pipe or spoon out golf-ball-sized portions. Bake as instructed above. Before serving, fill the puffs with cheese or a savory mousse.

## Profiteroles, Cream Puffs, and Éclairs

Reduce the total salt to ⅛ teaspoon and add 1 tablespoon of sugar to the water in the basic *pâte à choux* ingredients.

On a parchment- or Silpat-lined baking sheet, pipe or spoon out golf-ball-sized portions or, for éclairs, pipe out 4- to 5-inch logs. Place in an oven preheated to 425°F for 10 minutes, then reduce the heat to 350°F to complete their cooking, 10 to 20 minutes longer.

## *Parisienne Gnocchi*

The standard ratio for *pâte à choux* can be used for gnocchi, but I like to reduce the water in the basic *pâte à choux* ingredients to 6 ounces (or by 25 percent of whatever quantity you're making) for a more dense pasta. I also increase the salt to 1 teaspoon, and I stir in ¼ cup of grated Parmigiano-Reggiano after the eggs have been incorporated.

This dough itself can be augmented in any number of ways, with different flavors and seasonings. I first learned this preparation from Jeff Cerciello, then executive chef of the Bouchon restaurants. At Bouchon, the kitchen includes fresh herbs, mustard, and Comté cheese in the basic dough.

Spoon the *pâte à choux* into a pastry bag fitted with a ½-inch tip or into a sturdy plastic bag with a corner cut out. Pipe directly into simmering water, cutting the choux paste at 1-inch intervals. Cook for a minute or two after the gnocchi rise to the surface (bite into one to make sure they're cooked through), then remove them to a sheet tray lined with a dish towel to drain. Chill until ready to use or store in the freezer.

Since they freeze so well, a convenient way to handle these gnocchi is to pipe them out on a baking sheet lined with a Silpat or parchment paper; pipe rows lengthwise across the sheet. Either fit your bag with a star tip or drag the tines of a fork across their length to give them visual texture and sauce-carrying grooves. Place the sheet in the freezer until the *pâte à choux* is completely frozen. Remove from the freezer and line the frozen bars of *pâte à choux* on a cutting board and cut into ½-inch gnocchi. Work quickly to avoid allowing them to thaw and become sticky. Place in a sturdy plastic bag and return to the freezer until ready to use.

## Working with Cooked Gnocchi

These gnocchi, once they are poached and drained (they can be chilled for up to a day after being poached), are best sautéed in a small amount of butter. They develop a crisp brown exterior, and the additional color, texture, and flavor is desirable.

They can be combined with any seasonal ingredients on hand, or any variation on pasta that strikes you. And if nothing strikes you, consider the following, which are simply known pairings, ingredients that go well together (winter squash and sage, basil and tomatoes, and so on).

In spring and summer:

- *Ramps and roasted peppers.* Cut 1½ cups of fresh ramps and their greens into 2-inch pieces. Sauté them in olive oil and butter for 30 seconds. Add the cooked gnocchi and sauté until golden brown. Add 2 red bell peppers that have been roasted, peeled, seeded, and cut into strips. Garnish with fresh Parmigiano-Reggiano and torn leaves of parsley.
- *Basil, tomatoes, and garlic.* I don't know when this combination doesn't work—I've yet to encounter such a variation. Smash 4 cloves of garlic with the flat side of a knife and chop them to a paste. Briefly sauté the garlic and the cooked gnocchi in a mixture of butter and olive oil. Add a cup of diced tomatoes or halved cherry and pear tomatoes and ¼ cup of chopped basil. Heat through. Season with salt and pepper, divide among four plates, and garnish with basil chiffonade, about ¼ cup per plate.
- *Corn, bacon, and fava beans.* Sauté ¾ pound of diced bacon. Sauté ½ cup of diced onion in the rendered bacon fat and cook until translucent. Add the cooked gnocchi and sauté until golden brown. Add ¾ cup each of fresh corn and fava beans that have been boiled and shocked in ice water (or fresh lima beans or fresh soybeans). Finish with ¼ cup of cream and plenty of freshly cracked pepper.

In fall and winter:

- *Chicken and dumplings!* This dough makes perfect light, flavorful, satisfying dumplings for a chicken stew. Load the *pâte à choux* with tarragon and chives, pipe it or cut it or spoon it directly into a hearty chicken soup or a chicken stew and cook the dumplings until they float. Use the same method to make a thick chicken soup as you would for cream soups (page 115); don't puree, hold the cream, and add the dumplings just before serving. This is the perfect way to make a complete second meal of a roast chicken, using the carcass to make a stock and adding more aromatic vegetables and any reserved chicken from what was left over.

- *Butternut squash, sage, and brown butter.* This is a classic pairing that works especially well with gnocchi. Sauté 2 cups of diced butternut squash in some butter until tender. Add ¼ to ½ cup of torn sage leaves and 4 additional tablespoons of butter, along with the cooked gnocchi, raise the heat to medium-high, and cook until the gnocchi and butter are browned and the sage is thoroughly cooked.
- *Mushrooms, shallot, and spinach.* In a very hot pan, sauté mushrooms with salt and pepper in canola oil until they're nicely browned. Transfer to a plate and keep warm. Brown the cooked gnocchi in a little butter. In a separate pan, sweat ⅓ cup of thinly sliced shallots in a little butter until it's translucent. Turn the heat to high and add the spinach, tossing the spinach to wilt it. Season with salt and pepper as you're cooking it. When it's wilted, add ¼ cup of cream and stir to heat. Combine the gnocchi and spinach, add the mushrooms, toss well, divide among plates, and garnish with lemon zest.
- *Clams, white wine, garlic, and thyme.* Brown the cooked gnocchi in a little butter. In a pot, bring ½ cup of dry white wine to a simmer with 5 to 10 stems of thyme and 4 cloves of garlic smashed beneath the flat side of a knife. Add 1½ to 2 pounds of littleneck clams and cover the pot. Cook until the clams are steamed open, a couple of minutes. Divide the gnocchi among bowls and top with the clams. Pour the clam liquid through a fine-mesh strainer into a saucepan. Bring to a simmer, mount an ounce of butter into it, whisking until it's incorporated, and pour it over the gnocchi and clams. Garnish with rough-chopped flat-leaf parsley.

### Gnocchi à la Romaine

During my brief time as a clock-punching line cook at the Cleveland restaurant Sans Souci, where I worked grill, I was taught a variation of the *pâte à choux* gnocchi. Instead of its coming together in moments using AP flour, I made it like polenta using semolina flour, the sturdy stuff made from high-protein durum wheat. I'd rain the semolina into the liquid (milk, not water), and stir stir stir until it was cooked, then add some egg and nutmeg and cheese. I'd pour out the concoction onto a sheet pan, chill it overnight, and cut 3-inch rounds of it for service. (Because we were cutting rounds, there was always a lot of trim, which I compulsively devoured cold right there at my station—this is serious comfort food, none better, in fact.) Pickup was simple—it went onto a sizzle platter with some cheese on top, and into the oven until it was piping hot and the cheese was browned. But I could never understand why the chef, Claude Rodier, a disciple of Roger Vergé, called this stuff gnocchi. It wasn't until working on the *Bouchon* cookbook that I understood why. Until then, I figured he, nutty Frenchman, was simply using more of that creative naming the French are so adept at. This particular variation on the *pâte à choux* gnocchi is formally called gnocchi à la romaine, and is a great substitute for potatoes or polenta, with its rich, creamy texture and mild flavor. I called Chef Claude to discuss the preparation, and he said this was traditionally just gratinéed, perhaps with a béchamel or Mornay, but he could serve this with any number of dishes. Veal was common, a chop or a saltimbocca preparation. It would be excellent with a veal stew or a beef stew and would work well with fish. "Yes, fish, why not?" And he began to muse. "A bacon-wrapped monkfish . . . with chanterelles . . . and a red wine jus." And this excellent variation on the classic *pâte à choux*.

> 2 cups milk
> 2 ounces butter (½ stick)
> 2 teaspoons salt
> 4 ounces semolina
> Pepper and nutmeg to taste
> ¼ cup freshly grated Parmigiano-Reggiano
> 2 large egg yolks

In a medium saucepan combine the milk, butter, and salt and bring to a simmer over high heat. When the butter is melted, reduce the heat to medium and rain in the semolina while stirring with a wooden spoon until it's all incorporated. Continue stirring until the semolina is completely hydrated and cooked, about 10 minutes (the mixture should be rich and smooth). Remove the pan from the heat and season the gnocchi with pepper and nutmeg (add more salt if necessary). Stir in the Parmesan and yolks. Pour out into a 9-inch baking dish, or whatever you have, which should be lined with parchment paper, so that you have a layer about ¾ inch thick. Allow it to cool, then refrigerate uncovered until chilled.

The gnocchi will keep like this, well wrapped, for several days. When ready to use, simply remove the gnocchi from the pan to a cutting board, cut it into the desired shape (munch on the trim), top with cheese (Gruyère or Parmigiano-Reggiano, for example), and bake at 425°F until hot.

## Serving Gnocchi à la Romaine

The chilled sheet of gnocchi should be fairly stiff, allowing you to cut it into any shape you wish. At the restaurant, I used a 4-inch ring mold to cut pucks, which made for an elegant presentation but also created a lot of trim. For home preparations, you can simply cut them into rectangles so that there's no waste, or figure out some shape that reduces the amount of trim, such as diamonds or triangles.

The dough can be flavored in the way that mashed potatoes are, with roasted garlic, or you might stir in freshly minced chives and parsley, depending on how you intend to serve it and with what.

These gnocchi are hearty and can easily be the foundation for a vegetarian meal, swathed in abundant wild mushrooms that have been sautéed with some shallot and finished with butter or some stock and wine. And you might use a variation on the pairings suggested for the parisienne gnocchi (pages 50–51), creating a ragù on which to rest the gnocchi à la romaine.

Plain, it is an excellent side dish with braised meats, such as lamb shank or veal stew or beef short ribs, grilled lamb chops, veal chops, or pork tenderloin, or as a base for hearty fish such as sautéed grouper, halibut, or monkfish.

# BATTERS

Batter is dough you can pour, a dough with more liquid than solids. The liquid spreads the gluten out so that the network is fluid. Because the gluten is so spread out, batters don't hold air the way doughs do. Most flour-water mixtures, whether dough or batter, require some form of leavening, or what you wind up with is hardtack (pasta and some cookies are exceptions). To leaven batters, we usually rely on the egg, baking powder, and baking soda.

Much of baking, and especially batters, is predicated less on the ingredients than the *order* in which the ingredients are combined and the *way* they are combined. For instance, sugar, butter, eggs, and flour are the main ingredients in a cake batter, but the end result will differ depending on which mixing method you use. If, for instance, you combine the butter and sugar and beat them, then add the eggs and flour, you will have a dense rich pound cake. If you combine the exact same quantities of eggs and sugar first and beat them, then add the flour and the butter, you will have a light, airy, tender sponge cake. That's why batters are organized by the type of mixing method used, whether the creaming method (resulting in pound cake), foaming method (resulting in sponge cake),

*Lining your cake pan with parchment makes ▶ removing the cake easy and clean.*

straight mixing method (resulting in crepes, pancakes, muffins), or some combination or variation of these (a variety of different cakes).

This critical role of the mixing method means that while ratios are important with batters, they're less important to understand than the mixing method. Or rather, the ratios are variable; you can make that same pound cake using only half the butter and it will still be a pound cake (though a little bit cakier and less rich) provided you use the creaming method. And the skill with which the ingredients have been mixed can often make the difference between good and great.

What I like most about the batter ratios, though, is what they have to teach us about the similarities between the extensive variety of preparations, the impact of the proportions of fundamental ingredients. Batters are almost incestuously linked to one another and show an exceptionally delicate balance between one another. The loosest of the batters is crepe, and we move up with increasing proportions of flour to popover, pancake and fritter, muffin, cake, and so on in potentially infinite variations until you hit the point of the fulcrum and tip over into dough, *pâte à choux*, pasta, pie, cookie, and bread (in that order on the batter-dough continuum).

How is a crepe different from a popover? Popovers typically use half as much egg. How is a crepe different from a pancake? A pancake has more flour and less egg (and includes a chemical leavener and sometimes butter, which adds to the cakiness). How is a fritter

batter different from a pancake? A little more flour, but for most purposes you can use a basic thick pancake batter, without the butter, for fritters. But you could also call that kind of batter a muffin batter. How is a crepe different from a muffin? In the exact same way that it's different from a pancake, which is a muffin batter cooked in a skillet. How is a crepe different from sponge cake? The ingredients are similar in proportion, but instead of milk, butter is used, along with 1 part sugar. If you under-

◀ *Boon companions: the balloon whip and eggs.*

stand the creaming method versus the foaming method, you can begin to intuit what makes a cake, versus a muffin, versus a pancake, versus a popover, versus a crepe. They're all part of the same tree. And I think that people who are gifted pastry chefs have simply seen the crepe-cake continuum more clearly for longer, rather than seeing crepe equaling one set of instructions, cake another, and so have been able to improvise; they understand how small adjustments in fat, flour, egg, and sugar can result in satisfying nuances of lightness and delicacy or richness in flavor and texture. It's all one thing.

Which is why I love cooking. It's all one thing. Which is the ultimate comfort in a life fraught with uncertainty and questions. Which is why I don't fear dying. Which is what I'd put on my headstone if I thought being buried in the ground mattered: "It's all one thing." Which is why I love batters.

*Baked batters. Angel food cake, top, tends to sink ▶*
*in the middle and so it's often baked in a tube pan;*
*I improvise a tube pan by filling a springform pan*
*with the batter and pressing a glass into the center.*
*Muffin batter can be poured into a loaf pan for*
*sweet batter breads (bottom right), and this pound*
*cake was baked in a terrine mold.*

# Pound Cake
# and Sponge Cake

**Pound Cake = 1 part butter : 1 part sugar : 1 part egg : 1 part flour**

**Sponge Cake = 1 part egg : 1 part sugar : 1 part flour : 1 part butter**

I divide cakes, those we serve in wedges, often with some fat-rich or sweet icing, into two categories: with fat and without fat. Cakes with fat are sponge cakes (or a variant we call pound cake). They're rich and moist. Cake without fat (no butter, no yolks) are angel food cakes. These are very soft and delicate. While there are any number of variations on the cake—chiffon, génoise, angel, devil, pound, sponge, and so on—and ways of mixing the ingredients and how they might be leavened, understanding these two fundamental categories of cakes makes all cakes easier. Both types are very easy to prepare and should be part of your repertoire rather than your relying on the dry, chemically flavored boxed mixes.

Pound and sponge cake—they contain the exact same ingredients in the exact same quantities. The single most important lesson to learn in baking is revealed by this ratio for cake: in baking, the mixing method—that is, the order

*This dense, rich pound cake ▶ was made with equal parts egg, flour, sugar, and butter and was flavored with vanilla and the zest and juice of a lemon and a lime.*

in which the ingredients are combined—determines the end results as much as the ingredients.

It's especially clear in this ratio because these cakes contain the four cornerstone ingredients of the pastry kitchen in equal measure. Obviously, recipes vary in any number of degrees. Butter can be reduced by half or eliminated altogether. If you use the foaming method—whipping whole eggs until they're frothy before adding the remaining ingredients (see page 63)—you'll still get a good cake. If you want more rise and cakiness, you can double the amount of eggs. For still more rise, you can whip the whites separately and fold this into the batter. Often baking powder is included in the batter for leavening. But as a general rule, the equal parts by weight is solid provided you adhere to the proper mixing method.

Pound cake is perhaps the best-known recipe called by its ratio. One pound each of butter, sugar, egg, and flour are combined in that order using the creaming method, whipping the butter and sugar together first. But a perfect sponge cake can be achieved with those exact ingredients if you use the foaming method, whipping the eggs and sugar together first. Neither of these cakes requires the chemical leavening of baking powder.

The creaming method, typically used in some cakes, brownies, and cookies, refers to paddling sugar into butter, until the sugar is uniformly distributed and the butter has increased slightly in volume and become bright and pale. The butter changes because bubbles of air are being incorporated into the mixture. These air bubbles will expand and help to leaven the batter. Failing to develop enough air in your butter-sugar mixture can result in a dense, heavy finished product.

Next eggs are added, incrementally as they are incorporated into the butter-sugar mixture. At either point, in the creaming or the adding of eggs, the mixture can appear to break, not desirable but not the disaster it is in the sauce world. The batter should come back together when the dry ingredients are added.

When the eggs have been incorporated, the dry ingredients are folded, stirred, or paddled into the butter-sugar-egg mixture. If additional liquid is to be added, it's done here, often in between additions of the dry ingredients. Sometimes a chemical leavener, baking powder or baking soda, is added to the batter to increase leavening. (You could add yeast to this as the leavener, but then it would be brioche, not cake.)

And that's all there is to the creaming method. Sometimes recipes instruct you to "cream" sugar and egg yolks. This means do the same thing as you would if you were creaming sugar into butter to achieve similar effects, though it's not technically "creaming"—it's a variant of the "foaming" method (see sponge cake, page 63). Again, the most important stage is incorporating air into the sugar-butter mixture.

### Old-Fashioned Pound Cake (Creaming Method)

This is straight out of pioneer cooking, though it's a heck of a lot easier now given a little jolt of electricity and a standing mixer (not to mention a better understanding of the physics and chemistry of cooking). Harold McGee, in his *On Food and Cooking,* cites a pound cake recipe from Hannah Glasse, the eighteenth-century Englishwoman who wrote *The Art of Cookery* (1747), in which a pound of eggs is beaten into a pound of butter followed by flour—"beat it all well together for an hour with your hand, or a great wooden spoon."

Today's method is considerably easier and the cake, I would imagine, quite a bit lighter. Many pound cake recipes play fast and loose with the ratio, decreasing the flour for more moisture, increasing the sugar for sweetness and delicacy, increasing the eggs or altering the yolk to white proportions (Glasse's recipe calls for 6 eggs and 6 yolks).

I prefer the simplicity, flavor, and heft of the classic ratio, which results in a buttery, eggy cake that is delicious as is, excellent with a glaze, and beautiful when toasted for breakfast. It can be seasoned as you wish—with citrus juice and zest or with sweet spices such as cinnamon, ginger, and nutmeg. If you insist on reducing the fat and flavor, you can reduce the butter by any degree you wish up to 50 percent, and still have a good pound cake.

This recipe is for 1 lemon-lime pound cake and will fill a 9-inch loaf pan. It actually mixes better when doubled up to the pound ratio.

*8 ounces butter (2 sticks; at room temperature, ideally 65°F to*
*70°F), plus enough for buttering a loaf pan*
*8 ounces sugar*

*1 teaspoon salt*

*8 ounces eggs (4 large eggs plus 1 large yolk, ideally at room*
    *temperature), lightly whipped to combine*

*Juice and zest of 1 lemon*

*Juice and zest of 1 lime*

*1 teaspoon vanilla extract*

*8 ounces flour (about 1¾ cups)*

FOR THE CITRUS GLAZE

*1 tablespoon lemon juice*

*1 tablespoon lime juice*

*¼ cup sugar*

Preheat your oven to 325°F. Butter a 9-inch loaf pan.

Put the butter into the bowl of a standing mixer and beat it with the paddle attachment at medium speed for a minute. Add the sugar and salt and beat on medium-high until the butter becomes very pale and has increased in volume by about a third, 2 to 3 minutes. Add the eggs slowly so that they are gradually beaten into the batter, another minute or so. Add a tablespoon each of the lemon and lime juices, all the zest from the fruits, and the vanilla. Reduce the speed of the mixer to medium-low and add the flour. Mix only long enough to incorporate the flour. Pour the batter into your pan and bake for 1 hour, then test the interior with a paring knife or toothpick. When the blade comes out clean, remove the loaf pan and let it rest for 5 minutes or so; turn the cake out onto a rack to finish cooling.

Meanwhile, for the glaze, combine the citrus juices and sugar in a pan over medium-high heat and stir until the sugar is dissolved. Taste to check the sweet-sour balance and adjust as necessary. Brush the pound cake on all sides with the glaze.

YIELD: ONE 9-INCH POUND CAKE

## Sponge Cake (Foaming Method)

Sponge cake differs from pound cake in the way the ingredients are mixed. Rather than creaming the sugar into the butter, which results in lots of tiny air bubbles, whole eggs are whipped until they triple in volume, a process that results in lots and lots and lots of bigger bubbles (and as a result a lighter, fluffier cake). This can be done with cold eggs, or the sugar and eggs can be gently warmed over a water bath to dissolve the sugar and prime the eggs for their volume-tripling work, which is the method I prefer.

Once the eggs and sugar are foamed and additional flavor is added (vanilla, citrus), flour is folded into this foam, gently to avoid destroying the bubbles, followed by the melted butter. It's important that your flour be sifted. The author and television guy Alton Brown suggests combining dry ingredients in a food processor and pulsing them a few times in order to sift them, and this is an excellent method.

If there's one part of the ratio that is most variable, it's the quantity of butter added to your sponge cake. You don't have to use any butter at all. You can use only a fraction of the butter. But I use the full amount here to prove the point about mixing methods being the key to great baking, and because I am a butter advocate. It makes this sponge cake rich and delicious.

And that's all there is to fundamental cake baking. The only other critical part of the cake process is having your pans ready and your oven

*A sponge cake can be made* ▶ *with the same ingredients in the same proportion used to make pound cake, but you develop its airy crumb by whipping the eggs and sugar until the mixture is thick and frothy. You can add a teaspoon or two of baking powder if you wish for even more lift, but strictly speaking, chemical leavener is not necessary.*

hot. After you've developed the air bubbles in your mixture, the faster you get it all into your pan, the better.

I prefer baking these in a springform pan, which makes unmolding them easier, but cake pans are, of course, the customary method. With angel and sponge cakes, the sides of the pan shouldn't be greased, which helps the cake to maintain volume. The following recipe can be doubled to fill two 9-inch cake pans for a layer cake.

> *8 ounces eggs (4 large eggs plus 1 large yolk)*
> *8 ounces sugar*
> *1 teaspoon salt*
> *2 tablespoons lemon juice*
> *1 teaspoon vanilla extract*
> *2 teaspoons baking powder (optional)*
> *8 ounces flour (about 1¾ cups), sifted*
> *8 ounces butter (2 sticks), melted but cool*

Preheat your oven to 350°F.

Fill a pan, one large enough to contain the base of your mixing bowl, with a couple of inches of water and bring it to a gentle simmer as you scale your ingredients and ready your pan (either a springform pan or a cake pan lined with parchment). Combine the eggs, sugar, salt, lemon juice, and vanilla in the bowl of your standing mixer. Place the bowl over the simmering water and whisk until the eggs are warm, just above body temperature, and the sugar has begun to melt, about a minute or so. (Remember, you're just warming the eggs to facilitate foaming them, not cooking them; some people simply use room-temperature eggs.) Place the mixing bowl in its stand and with the whisk attachment, whip the eggs and sugar on high until the eggs have tripled in volume, a few minutes. Remove the bowl from the mixer. If using, combine the baking powder with the flour. Fold in the sifted flour just until you can't see it anymore, then fold in the butter, and pour the batter into the pan. Bake for 30 to 45 minutes, until a paring knife or toothpick inserted into the center comes out clean.

YIELD: ONE 9- BY 2-INCH LAYER OF SPONGE CAKE

# Angel Food Cake

**Angel Food Cake = 3 parts egg white : 3 parts sugar : 1 part flour**

Angel food cake is a meringue to which a small amount of flour has been added to give it a little structure. Given a scale and an electric mixer, angle food cake couldn't be easier: whip egg whites and half the sugar to soft peaks, adding some flavor (vanilla, lemon, sweet spices), fold in the flour and the remaining sugar gently, and bake. Easy *if* you know how to mix it properly. The key to a tall and fluffy cake, as opposed to one that has sunken and become dense and chewy, is not the ratio (doubling the flour, for instance, will not substantially change your cake), but rather the mixing of the egg whites to just the right volume and no more. This means the difference between a good-looking but dense cake and a cake that lives up to its name. The egg-white-and-sugar mixture should not be whipped feverishly; it should be whipped on medium to medium-high in order to prevent overmixing. If it's whipped too hard and becomes too stiff, it won't rise properly. There's a point in the mixing when it's white and fluffy but still pourable, and then a few moments later it's just stiff

*An angel food cake batter is composed of egg whites* ▶ *and sugar and rises considerably when it's baked, as the millions of air bubbles created by vigorous mixing expand. A glass will be pressed into the center of this pan to improvise a tube pan. Don't use a handblown glass or a glass with visible bubbles or it may break.*

enough that it won't quite pour but neither is it so stiff that it holds a stiff peak. That's the moment you want to stop mixing. At this point you've developed plenty of air bubbles, but have not made the egg white resistant to the expansion that will happen when the air bubbles warm and when the water in the egg white vaporizes.

Good *mise en place* is critical in cake making. Make sure your oven is already hot, that your cake pan is ready, and your flour-sugar mixture is sifted (an easy, quick way to do this is to pulse it in a food processor with the blade attachment), so that you lose as few of those air bubbles as possible. Use cake flour, a low-protein, finely grained flour, which results in a more tender product. Fold the flour-sugar mixture into the meringue thoughtfully—by "folding," I mean flipping the batter over on itself using a rubber spatula, rather than stirring, again to avoid losing air bubbles. Pour or scoop the batter gently into the pan and bake for about 40 minutes, depending on your pan. Angel food cakes are often cooked in tube pans, but because the lack of fat and abundance of sugar creates a situation in which the cake sticks to the pan—fat would compromise the cake— I prefer using a springform pan (with a glass in the center if I want a tube shape). Alternately, line your pan with parchment paper.

When the cake is cooked, it should be allowed to cool upside down for a minimum of an hour to let the delicate sugar-protein network completely set before you unmold it (1½ hours is better).

## Angel Food Cake

This cake is delicious all by itself if you flavor it well. Vanilla is usually a good idea here, and while there is some cream of tartar, which is simply powdered acid that helps stabilize the egg-white foam and whiten the mixture, I also like to add some lemon juice for additional seasoning. Salt also helps to enhance flavor and stabilize the foam. The plain cake can be combined with any number of garnishes. A light icing of flavored whipped cream is delicious and elegant, as are macerated berries or a sabayon made from leftover yolks.

*12 ounces egg whites (9 to 11 large egg whites)*
*12 ounces sugar*

*4 ounces cake flour*
*3-fingered pinch of salt (about ½ teaspoon)*
*½ teaspoon cream of tartar*
*1 tablespoon freshly squeezed lemon juice*
*1 teaspoon vanilla extract*

Preheat your oven to 350°F.

Measure out the egg whites in the mixing bowl and place in the mixer using the whisk attachment. Combine half the sugar and the flour in a food processor. Beat the egg whites on medium for a minute or so, then add the salt, cream of tartar, lemon juice, and vanilla and increase the mixing speed to medium-high. Once the foam has been established and the mixture is opaque, begin drizzling in the remaining plain sugar. Continue mixing until the sugar is incorporated and the foam just passes the pourable stage. It will hold a weak peak.

Pulse the sugar-flour two or three times to aerate it, and sprinkle it over the meringue as you fold the meringue with a rubber spatula. Continue to sprinkle and gently fold the mixture over on itself until all the remaining sugar-flour has been incorporated. Pour into your pan—this recipe will fill a 9-inch springform pan or 9-inch tube pan—and bake for 30 to 50 minutes (it's done when a skewer or a toothpick inserted into the center comes out clean).

Invert the pan onto a rack, a bottle, or an inverted glass, depending on your pan, and allow the cake to cool for 1½ hours before removing it from the pan.

YIELD: ONE 9-INCH CAKE

# Quick Cakes

**Quick Bread = 2 parts flour : 2 parts liquid : 1 part egg : 1 part butter**

**Muffin = 2 parts flour : 2 parts liquid : 1 part egg : 1 part butter**

**Pancake = 2 parts liquid : 1 part egg : ½ part butter: 2 parts flour**

**Fritter = 2 parts flour : 2 parts liquid : 1 part egg**

**Popover = 2 parts liquid : 1 part egg : 1 part flour**

Quick cakes, called batter breads or quick breads, all use the same mixing method, often called the straight mixing method, and differ primarily in the flour-to-liquid ratio. A quick bread is composed of cake batter ingredients that are stirred together and leavened with baking powder. Muffins are quick breads baked in cups. Muffin batter is different from popover batter only in that there's twice as much flour and usually includes baking powder. Popovers get their leavening from the cooking method. They're simply custards cooked at a high temperature with some flour thrown in. Or

*Muffins are essentially flavored pancake batter* ▶
*and can be baked in muffin shapes or in a loaf pan*
*for a batter bread; they can be sweet or savory, and*
*garnishes—berries, diced fruit or vegetables, nuts,*
*spices—are limited only by your imagination.*

you might think of a popover as a loose form of hot baked *pâte à choux*; they have a similar leavening and interior structure. A muffin batter is essentially what holds abundant garnish together to be fried into fritters. Pancakes are really just thin muffins.

Because these flour-liquid-egg concoctions are so intriguingly interlaced, and because they are all mixed the same way (that is, the ingredients are simply stirred together), I'll treat them all together here.

All of them except the popover require baking powder for leavening. The popover achieves its leavening from the steam release in high heat. Recipes vary considerably on how much baking powder to use. I've found that a good working rule is 1 teaspoon per 4 ounces of flour (a scant cup), or 5 grams for every 110 grams of flour. If you want a little more leavening, for fluffy pancakes, you can double this proportion. (Baking soda will do the same leavening, given sufficient acid to react with it, but I prefer double-acting baking powder, which contains its own acid, also releases gas when heated, and is a more consistent leavener.)

Another variable is sweetness. Most quick cake preparations are sweet. But the type of muffin you're making should determine the level of sweetness. If you have a lot of sweet garnish, banana or sweet apple, or if your cake or muffin is to be served with a very sweet sauce or accompaniment, you might want your batter somewhat less sweet. Popovers can take a little sugar but are delicious with none at all. But a good rule of thumb for muffins and cakes and pancakes is to add as much sugar as butter.

The wonderful thing about quick breads and popovers is that they're so easy: stir the ingredients together (not too much or too vigorously, or they can become tough) and bake. You can *think* about a quick bread, then have it in your hungry little mouth in under an hour. And pancakes, retrieving the ingredients takes longer than actually mixing them, given a bowl and a scale—they can go from idea to the table in 15 minutes. So batters are an incredibly valuable skill to have at your fingertips.

Using a ratio makes the cooking that much faster. When using batter ratios, I almost always make ingredients relative to the quantity of egg, since large eggs are 2 ounces. So I would make a 2-egg popover batter (8 ounces milk, 4 ounces flour), which will give you nearly 2 cups of batter for 6 standard popovers. If I'm just making pancakes for my son and no one else, I'll do a 1-egg pancake batter (4 ounces milk, 4 ounces flour, 1 ounce melted butter, and a teaspoon of baking powder). For a moderate batch of muffins,

10 or so, use a 2-egg batter (8 ounces flour, 8 ounces milk, 4 ounces butter, 4 ounces sugar).

Once you have the ratio, variations are infinite.

## *Basic Quick Bread/Muffin Batter*

All these recipes are made by combining the dry ingredients and the wet ingredients separately, then combining the two and stirring just to combine.

*8 ounces flour*
*4 ounces sugar*
*1 teaspoon salt*
*2 teaspoons baking powder*
*8 ounces milk*
*4 ounces eggs (2 large eggs)*
*4 ounces butter (1 stick), melted*

Preheat your oven to 350°F.

Combine the flour, sugar, salt, and baking powder (if your baking powder is pebbly, push it through a strainer). In a quart measuring cup or bowl, combine the milk, eggs, and butter. With a whisk or a hand blender, whisk or blend the mixture until the eggs are uniformly distributed. Add the dry ingredients. Whisk just to combine. If you're adding additional garnish, such as citrus zest or fruit, do so now.

Pour the batter into muffin tins or a loaf pan (butter or spray your vessel with vegetable oil if it isn't made of nonstick material). Bake for about 30 minutes, or as much as 50 minutes for a loaf, until the blade of a paring knife inserted in the center comes out clean.

YIELD: 10 MUFFINS

Variations and Types of Quick Bread and Muffins

- *Blueberry is a standard for a reason.* Blueberries' sweet-sour juiciness makes for extraordinary muffins. Same with raspberries. And blackberries (though these can require more sugar; taste them to see how tart they are).
- *Cranberry-orange.* Add dried cranberries, and replace one-quarter of the milk with fresh orange juice. Add the zest of 1 or 2 oranges. You can plump the cranberries in orange juice or Grand Marnier for variations on the cranberry-orange pairing. Or don't use cranberries, but flavor the batter with Myers's rum and make a Myers's rum glaze (equal parts rum and sugar, heated until the sugar is dissolved).
- *Apple-cinnamon.* Use brown sugar instead of white, add a teaspoon of cinnamon and a cup of diced Granny Smith apple.
- Of course, *lemon–poppy seed muffins* are excellent standards as well.
- Reduce the liquid by 2 ounces, add a cup of mashed bananas, and brown the butter for *banana bread*.
- Don't neglect the options of savory breads and muffins. You might add a tablespoon of curry powder, ¼ teaspoon of cayenne, and ½ cup each of diced red and green peppers, omit the sugar, and replace the butter with browned butter.
- For corn muffins, replace three-quarters of the flour with cornmeal. Add a cup of corn and 3 diced jalapeños as garnish.

*Basic Pancake Batter*

What I like about a pancake ratio is that you can tailor the amount according to how many people you want to feed, even if you just want to feed yourself. Also, you can vary it to your own taste, adding more or less liquid for thinner or thicker pancakes. Buttermilk or homemade yogurt can be measured as half the liquid for a more complex flavor. You can also replace 25 percent of the flour with cornmeal, whole wheat flour, or other ground cereals or grains for differing flavors and textures. These are standard pancakes, flavored with a little sugar and vanilla. I like to cook them on a film of bacon fat, which gives them a crisp crust.

WET INGREDIENTS

*8 ounces milk*
*2 large eggs*
*2 ounces butter (½ stick), melted*
*1 teaspoon vanilla extract*

DRY INGREDIENTS

*8 ounces flour (1⅛ to 1½ cups)*
*2 tablespoons sugar*
*2 teaspoons baking powder*
*1 teaspoon salt*

Combine the wet ingredients in a bowl and whisk until they are thoroughly combined.

Combine the dry ingredients (press the baking powder through a strainer if it's pebbly).

Combine the wet and dry ingredients and whisk or stir until the batter is smooth. This ratio results in a fairly thick batter, and thick, cakey pancakes. If you like them thinner, add 1 or 2 ounces of milk.

Cook on a lightly oiled surface, griddle or pan, over medium heat until done.

YIELD: ABOUT EIGHT 4-INCH PANCAKES

*I like a thick batter that results in a cakey pancake.* ▶
*If you poured this pancake batter over fresh corn and some spicy seasonings and then dropped spoonfuls of the corn into hot oil, you would have delicious fritters.*

## Basic Fritter Batter

Every time I make fritters, I ask myself why I don't make them more often. Crisp and tender, sweet and spicy. A fritter batter, which is a muffin batter without the butter, is a vehicle, like a crepe or a dumpling, for a tasty main garnish and seasoning, whether corn or clam or apple or zucchini. Use just enough batter to hold the garnish together. The following batter will be enough to bind about 2 cups of garnish. In addition to altering the fritter batter with spices and fresh herbs, you can also enhance the fritter's flavor by changing the liquid for savory fritters from milk to stock or beer; you can add citrus juices as part of the liquid (orange for apple fritters, lime for corn fritters), or, if you want to keep the flavors of the batter very clean, you can simply use water. The only thing to be concerned with when choosing a garnish is how much moisture the garnish has; very moist ingredients such as eggplant and mushroom may steam after the fritter is removed from the fat and make the fritter soggy rather than crisp.

Fritters make a great canapé, in which case you would want to serve them with some sort of dipping sauce. And, combining both starch and vegetable as they do, fritters make an excellent side dish—spicy corn fritters with grilled chicken or zucchini fritters with baked or

sautéed fish, for instance. They almost always benefit from a sprinkling of coarse salt and are best served piping hot.

*4 ounces flour (about ¾ cup)*
*½ teaspoon salt*
*1 teaspoon baking powder*

◄ *Fritters, made with muffin/pancake batter minus the butter and including appropriate seasonings (chilli powder, curry, cinnamon, fresh herbs), are easy to make and fun to eat. Crispness is part of their pleasure, so serve them immediately after you cook them, or they can become soggy.*

*4 ounces milk (or water, juice, or stock)*
*2 ounces egg (1 large egg)*

Combine the flour, salt, and baking powder (if your baking powder is chunky, push it through a strainer). Combine the milk (or other liquid) and the egg and whisk until the egg is uniformly dispersed. Add the flour mixture to the liquid and whisk until uniformly combined.

Prepare your interior garnish, such as diced apple or corn, and so on. Pour just enough fritter batter over the garnish to coat and hold it together.

Panfry by the spoonful in hot vegetable or canola oil until golden brown and cooked through, a few minutes per side.

YIELD: 8 LARGE FRITTERS

## TYPES OF FRITTERS

- *Curried pea and onion.* Make a standard fritter batter adding 2 teaspoons curry powder, 1 teaspoon turmeric, 1 teaspoon cumin, and ½ teaspoon cayenne. Mix the batter with 1 cup of peas (frozen are okay for this; if you're going to buy or grow and shell fresh peas, and I hope you will when they're in season, eat them boiled, with a little butter and salt or pureed as soup) and ¾ cup small-diced onion. This can be served with yogurt, minced shallot, and garlic and lemon juice dipping sauce.
- *Spicy corn fritters.* Make a standard fritter batter adding 1 teaspoon coriander, 1 teaspoon cumin, 1 teaspoon black pepper, ½ teaspoon chipotle powder (or smoked paprika or cayenne), and ¼ cup of chopped cilantro. Mix the batter with 2 cups of fresh corn and 2 chopped scallions. Serve with a squeeze of lime juice and cilantro leaves or with a lime-shallot mayonnaise dipping sauce (see Lemon-Shallot Mayonnaise, page 172).
- *Zucchini fritters.* Make a standard batter with the zest of 2 lemons, a tablespoon of lemon juice, and ½ teaspoon of cayenne. Combine with 2 cups of diced zucchini (central column of seeds discarded). Serve with salt and feta cheese and torn parsley.
- *Beer batter fritters.* Make a standard batter using a good pale ale as

your liquid and ½ teaspoon of black pepper. Combine with a cup each of diced zucchini and diced onion. Or dip onion rings or zucchini batons in the batter and fry. Serve with a squeeze of lemon and parsley.

- *Apple fritters.* Make a standard fritter batter with 2 egg yolks, 2 teaspoons cinnamon, and ¼ teaspoon freshly grated nutmeg. Whip the 2 egg whites to soft peaks and fold into the batter. Dip slices of crisp Fuji or Granny Smith apples in the batter and fry. Dust with cinnamon sugar or powdered sugar. Serve with ice cream or use pastry cream (see page 215) as a dipping sauce. Or sauté diced apples in butter and add to the fritter batter.

- *Peach fritters.* Make a standard fritter batter, reducing the quantity of liquid by one-quarter, and adding 1 teaspoon freshly ground black pepper. Toss with 2 cups of peeled, diced peaches. Dust with powdered sugar; top with lemon zest and torn mint.

- *Salt cod fritters.* Make a standard fritter batter using fish stock as your liquid (or milk, if you wish). Combine with 2 cups of diced or shredded salt cod (reconstituted in several changes of water over 24 hours). Serve with a squeeze of lemon and sage leaves sautéed in butter until crisp.

### Basic (but Amazing) Popovers

They're just too cool. This slack batter of flour, egg, and milk goes into a little cup into a very hot oven and a half hour later, *poof!*, a transformation as dramatic as popcorn. It puffs for the same reason—the steam—that gougères puff. Delicious, so, so easy, and yet they seem to be scarce in a home kitchen now reliant on boxed cake mix, bread machines, and Pop-Tarts.

Popovers are commonly served sweet, often as a breakfast dish. Their crisp exterior and warm creamy interior lend themselves to sweet preparations. But you can just as easily serve a popover with beef. Yorkshire pudding is nothing more than a popover batter, cooked in piping-hot beef fat. But a popover would work with any meat. It's soft as a Parker House roll and could be served just like one. You don't have bread but want to serve some with dinner? Make a few popovers (the quantities here will only be enough for 2 to 4 portions; double or triple them as needed). You could top them with Comté cheese or Parmigiano-Reggiano and serve them as a canapé (like gougères). They're delicious for breakfast with marmalade or preserves, of course; serve dusted with powdered sugar and with a little crème fraîche. And they would work great as a dessert (not unlike the gougère cousin, the profiterole), served hot, dusted with cinnamon sugar, with warm ganache and ice cream.

They're very forgiving and some people recommend starting them in a cold oven. I find the best volume and the most drama is achieved by pouring the batter into a hot vessel with hot flavorful fat. I recommend popover pans because their narrow base encourages a dramatic eruption, especially if you fill the pan to the top, which I like to do, though you can fill them only partway for smaller popovers. You don't need a proper pan to make them. They cook beautifully in ramekins and muffin tins, and some have suggested cooking them in ovenproof coffee mugs. You could cook them in a skillet if you wanted to. Many people make Yorkshire pudding right in the pan that the beef was cooked in, while the beef rests, so that it picks up all the fat and the juices that have caramelized in the pan.

You can put garnish in the popover batter—finely diced apple, grated Comté cheese, herbs if serving with savory dishes—but these tend to inhibit a great rise, which is much of the pleasure of a popover. So I don't recommend this, but instead recommend adding flavors after cooking— sprinkling with cheese during the last moments of baking; serving with some hot diced apple sautéed with butter and brown sugar, or simply with some sweet butter and honey.

> *8 ounces milk*
> *4 ounces eggs (2 large eggs)*
> *4 ounces flour (a scant cup)*
> *About 1 teaspoon salt to taste*
> *2 ounces butter (½ stick), melted, or canola oil*

*Like* pâte à choux, *popovers achieve their extraordinary* ▶
*rise when water vaporizes and makes them puff.*

Place a popover pan in your oven and preheat the oven to 450°F.

Combine the milk and eggs and whisk until they're uniformly combined. Add the flour and salt and stir until combined. Allow the batter to sit for a half hour (or longer), for the flour to bloom (or hydrate).

Remove the pan from the oven; put a couple of teaspoons of butter in each cup of the popover pan. Fill each cup with batter and bake for 10 minutes, then reduce the heat to 375°F, and continue baking until done, 20 to 30 minutes longer.

Serve straight from the oven with preserves, jams, or simply some good honey and butter.

YIELD: 2 TO 4 POPOVERS

## Tempura Batter

Vegetables and shellfish can be extraordinary dipped in a light batter and deep-fried. But they can also be leaden and oily. Tempura is a Japanese preparation, said to have been transported from Portugal in the seventeenth century, that can be prepared with great nuance and finesse. Batters are mixed *à la minute,* their thickness dependent on the item being fried. The traditional Japanese recipe uses wheat flour and contains egg. Some recipes call for yolks, others simply all-purpose flour or self-rising flour (flour with baking powder and salt added).

I believe the key to a great tempura is lightness and crispness. An easy way to achieve this, and here is how it differs from a fritter batter or any other batter, for that matter, is to make a batter low in gluten, the protein in flour that makes a dough or batter elastic. The way to reduce the gluten is to use a pure starch, such as cornstarch, as part of your dry mixture, and to use a low-gluten flour, cake flour, for the rest. You can experiment with what proportions you prefer, but I like a 3 to 1 combination (by volume or weight)—3 parts cake flour : 1 part cornstarch, adding about ½ teaspoon each of baking powder and of salt per cup (5 ounces) of flour/starch.

You can use water, but many like the effect of using sparkling water with the batter for additional lift. Another option is to use a good beer instead of soda water—this is especially good for onion rings or batons of zucchini. Another important step in achieving crispness is to mix the batter immediately before using, so that the starch doesn't absorb the water but rather the water is allowed to cook out quickly, leaving a very crisp light crust. The batter should be mixed to the consistency of heavy cream, and some small lumps are fine. The batter is best cold for maximum viscosity, and the item to be fried—shrimp, say, or zucchini—should be floured so that the wet batter adheres evenly to the dry surface.

Make a basic tempura mixture of ¾ cup cake flour, ¼ cup cornstarch, ½ teaspoon baking powder, and ½ teaspoon salt. When your oil is hot, add enough cold seltzer water to the tempura mixture to achieve a loose batter the consistency of heavy cream. Dip your items in the batter, cook them at once in 350°F oil, and serve them immediately.

Some excellent items to fry this way are shrimp, zucchini, onions, bell peppers, and mushrooms, but other vegetables are excellent as well and can yield interesting shapes and textures—green beans, batons of fennel, thin wedges of cabbage, slices of cauliflower, whole or halved garlic cloves. Tempuras are usually served with a soy-based dipping sauce with a good balance of saltiness, sweetness, and acidity. Japanese dipping sauces typically include soy, mirin, and dashi. But for an easy, satisfying dipping sauce, combine 2 tablespoons soy sauce, 1 teaspoon rice wine vinegar, ½ teaspoon sugar, and 1 teaspoon grated ginger.

# Crepe

**Crepe = 1 part liquid : 1 part egg : ½ part flour**

Crepes are a vehicle for foods and flavors used in cuisines throughout the world and can be served at any point in the meal, filled with savory ingredients or sweet. When chefs look for vehicles, they find that the crepe is one of the best. The batter itself can contain aromatic ingredients in addition to the structural ones. Herbs, chopped vegetables, sugar, vanilla, all work well in crepe batter. A crepe can be very thin and delicate, or it can be hearty and thick. Of course, if it gets too thick, then it's a pancake and not a crepe. Generally, the crepe is distinguished by its thinness and its delicacy.

A crepe always contains a starch, usually some kind of flour—though some Asian crepes include dried beans—and a water-based liquid, but not always egg. In Western cuisine, a crepe is milk, egg, and flour simply combined, then allowed to rest so that the flour hydrates. The batter is then poured into a pan just to coat the bottom. A general working ratio is equal volumes of milk, egg, and flour. The best ratio, though, is a weight ratio, which reduces the flour quantity somewhat, 1 part milk : 1 part egg : ½ part flour (a cup of flour weighs between 4 and 6 ounces). Both ratios work well and act as a starting

*Crepes can be papery thin or substantial depending* ▶
*on how much liquid you add to the batter. I prefer*
*them a little thicker so they have some bite and sub-*
*stantiality along with what's wrapped inside.*

point for whatever type of crepe you'd like to make, more liquid or less egg for a thinner crepe, for instance.

Any water-based liquid can be used in a crepe batter. Water is fine and results in an egg-noodle-like crepe. Milk adds some flavor. Cream adds richness. For sweet crepes, a juice such as orange juice works well. If you're making crepes to contain a savory filling, stock is an excellent liquid to use and will add a more complex backdrop than water or milk to the finished dish.

### Basic Crepes, for Savory or Sweet Fillings

I use weights here in keeping with the ratio, but it's all right to measure equal volumes of milk, egg, and flour, which will amount to a little more flour than a batter made according to the ratio—½ cup of each will make six 2-ounce crepes. It's a good idea to let the batter rest to allow the flour to hydrate and absorb the liquid.

Crepe pans are lovely to have and to use and require less fat for cooking the crepe, resulting in a lighter crepe. A well-seasoned cast-iron pan works well, too. A clean stainless-steel pan will suffice. The reason crepe pans, seasoned cast-iron pans, and nonstick pans are preferable to steel is that, with steel, you need to have a good film of butter or oil in your pan to prevent the crepe from sticking, which can make the crepe a little oily. Crepes are best when they're light and dry. Choose a pan with a basin the size you want your finished crepe to be. Two ounces of batter in a 5-inch pan will result in a crepe twice as thick as 2 ounces poured into a 9-inch pan. Crepes can be made as thick or as thin as you wish.

> 8 ounces milk
> 8 ounces eggs (4 large eggs)
> 4 ounces flour (a scant cup)
> Salt (optional)
> Sugar (optional)
> Vanilla extract (optional)

Combine the ingredients and blend with a whisk or hand blender until they're uniformly combined. A pinch of salt is always good no matter what you're using the crepes for, but if you're going savory, you can add ½ teaspoon (and can replace the milk with chicken stock, if you wish). If you're making sweet crepes, add 1 tablespoon of sugar and, if you wish, ½ teaspoon of vanilla. Let the batter rest for ½ hour or, covered in the refrigerator, up to a day. Heat your pan over medium heat. If you have a well-seasoned crepe pan or cast-iron pan, you need only put some vegetable oil on a paper towel and wipe the surface. If you are using stainless steel, swirl a teaspoon of butter in the pan to coat the bottom. Pour in just enough batter to coat the bottom as you tip and tilt the pan. Allow it to cook untouched until it's set, a minute or so. Then gently turn the crepe and briefly cook the other side. If after cooking the crepe, you would like it to be thinner, add ¼ cup of milk or more to the batter until you've got the consistency you like.

Remove the crepes to a rack as you make more. Crepes can be used immediately or they can be allowed to cool. When they're cool, stack them, cover, and refrigerate until you're ready to use them.

YIELD: SIX 2-OUNCE CREPES

## A Few of the Many Ways to Use Crepes

- Crepes are an excellent way to make leftover food elegant. If, for instance, you have leftover pulled pork or braised pot roast or beef stew, a new dinner is moments away given some crepes. Simply heat the food (and if the meat is big, such as pot roast, shred or cut it up so that it will fit into the crepe), roll it in a crepe, and top it with some of the braising liquid and some cheese and bake it until the cheese is melted.
- Alter the liquid. Juices and stocks can replace the milk in a standard crepe batter.
- Thomas Keller at the French Laundry has become famous for his lobster tail poached in butter, a great item for one of the country's finest four-star restaurants. This dish left him with abundant meat from the knuckles of all those lobsters. How could he serve these delicious but inelegant and oddly shaped chunks of lobster? His answer was to enfold them in a chive-embellished crepe, a little

circular bundle, rest it on a simple carrot sauce, and put a tiny salad of dressed pea greens on top. The same idea can be applied to any trim—say you had chunks of lamb left over from butterflying a leg, or scraps from trimming and cleaning a beef tenderloin. These visually unappealing and irregularly shaped bits can't really be served as they are, but you can wrap them in a crepe.

- That same leftover chicken that you were going to use in a chicken potpie or a chicken empanada can just as easily be rolled in a crepe, napped with sauce, and baked.
- Braise duck legs with plenty of aromatic vegetables and stock or water. Fill the crepe with the shredded meat. Strain and reduce the liquid, adding some wine and some butter, some *beurre manié* (page 121), for an elegant sauce, and top the crepe with a small salad of watercress lightly dressed with a vinaigrette.
- Any confited meats, such as duck confit or pork confit, are delicious in a crepe.
- Crepes are a great way to serve loose sausage.
- Think of common sandwich pairings and use the crepe as the vehicle rather than bread, such as ham and cheese: julienne some ham, mix it with some sautéed onions, roll the mixture in a crepe dressed with some mayonnaise and mustard, top with Swiss cheese, and bake until hot inside and the cheese is melted. Do crepes Philly cheesesteak style, thin slices of beef and topped with cheddar cheese. Or like a Reuben sandwich, corned beef and cabbage on the inside, topped with Swiss and baked.
- Sauté a pound of spinach with a tablespoon of minced shallot, some salt and pepper, and a few gratings of nutmeg until it's completely wilted; add ¼ cup of cream and cook until the cream is thickened. Roll the mixture in 4 to 6 crepes for an excellent vegetarian dish that's more substantial than simply creamed spinach.

Crepes are great as the vehicle for sweets.

- Fill with lemon curd (see page 28) and top with honey and crème fraîche.

- Spread crepes with raspberry jam, fold or roll, and top with powdered sugar.
- Make a dozen-layer crepe cake by spreading 12 crepes with jam or lemon curd (see page 28) and stacking one on top of the other and slicing it in wedges to serve.
- Sauté apple and brown sugar in butter until it's bubbling hot, wrap the mixture in a crepe, and dust with powdered sugar.
- Sauté bananas in butter and brown sugar. When the mixture is bubbling and hot, add a shot of rum, roll it in a crepe, and top with chocolate sauce (see page 221).
- Spread a layer of Nutella on hot crepes, fold into a triangle, and dust with sugar.
- Make a syrup of orange juice, sugar, and zest and a squeeze of lemon juice, adding a shot of Grand Marnier or cognac at the end. Reheat the crepes in the syrup, fold into triangles, and serve, adding more of the liqueurs and flaming them, if you wish, in the style of crepes suzette.

# PART TWO

# Stocks
# and the Amazing Things
# They Allow You to Do

# Stocks

**Stock = 3 parts water : 2 parts bones**

When I began this book, I started with stocks. They are, after all, *le fond de la cuisine,* the foundation upon which all else rests. So much of great cooking and soulful dishes begins with stock, the extraction, distillation, and concentration of *flavor*. And yet, does one really need ratios for stock? Or any of the preparations you use for stock? So much is done by eye. And, unlike in baking, small variations in ingredients in stocks and soups and sauces don't make or break the dish.

But how could I not include stock? Chef Hestnar had a column for it in his ratios, the sheet that inspired this book. Moreover, it may be the most commonly avoided preparation in American home kitchens, even though it's the single preparation that might elevate a home cook's food from decent to spectacular. How could a book that intended to address the fundamentals of cooking and baking ignore stock and what you can do with it? If anything, the power of ratios is about having variations at your fingertips, how possessing one small bit of crystalline information can open up a world of practical applications. Well, that's what stock is. So if I can convince anyone to make a little stock instead

*Straining stocks well is one of the most important ▶ steps in their creation. Stocks should be strained through cloth for the clearest, cleanest taste possible.*

of opening a can of factory-made "broth," this little interlude will have been worth it.

The truth is, stocks can be made quickly in small quantities. Indeed, much of the cooking we do involves stock making without actually calling it that. Anytime you add liquid to vegetables and meat and heat it, you're making stock whether or not you want to recognize it as such. In the roasted chicken with *fines herbes* (page 123), adding water is in effect a way of making your own quick stock in a matter of minutes. Water works like a charm, is always available, and costs a fraction of one cent, which is why I'm an advocate of using water instead of canned "broth" in recipes calling for small quantities of it. Or if you must use large quantities of the canned stuff, enhance it by first adding to it some onion and carrot and some fresh thyme.

I felt compelled to confess this dilemma before jumping into stocks and stock-related ratios. Stock is important.

## Foundations

To reiterate: if there's one preparation that separates a great home cook's food from a good home cook's food, it's stock. Stock is the ingredient that most distinguishes restaurant cooking from home cooking. Stocks are simply infused water, but they're a preparation that couldn't be more valuable to the home cook.

Stocks are infinitely variable and can be adjusted to virtually any kind of strength and body depending on your needs, so strictly speaking, a ratio here is more of a guide than a rule. You can make perfectly good stock using a 2 : 1 ratio and may *need* to do that depending on your quantity of bones and the size of your pot. A 1 : 1 ratio will result in a very strongly flavored, gelatinous stock (gelatin is what gives the stock body, a sense of being substantial in the mouth; if stock feels like water in the mouth, it has no body). But with this ratio, sometimes the bones are not all covered, which is the main concern with regard to the quantity of water. So for almost any stock, and generally speaking, a good ratio of water to main ingredient is 3 : 2 by weight. So if you're making chicken stock, that's 2 pounds of chicken bones and 3 pounds of water; for vegetable stock, 2 pounds of chopped vegetables and 3 pounds of water.

Water, of course, has an exact volume-to-weight relationship, so 3 pounds translate to 48 ounces or 6 cups. "A pint's a pound the world round," as the saying goes: 16 ounces according to your measuring cup should weigh 1 pound according to your scale; if it doesn't, there may be something wrong with your scale. This is an important fact in the kitchen—any ingredient such as water, one that has an equal volume-to-weight ratio, can be measured either in a volume measure or on a scale. Others, such as flour, are best measured by weight.

The rest of the ingredients in a stock aren't unessential or optional; you need onions and carrots—a meat stock won't have nearly the depth, complexity, and sweetness without these aromatic vegetables and can even have an unpleasant bony flavor—but peppercorns, bay leaf, thyme, and sweet vegetables don't need to be a hard-and-fast part of the ratio because they are so variable. Nevertheless, a working proportion is that your aromatic vegetables should equal about 20 percent of the total weight of bones and water. If you have 2 pounds of chicken bones and 3 pounds of water, you'd want to add roughly a pound of onion, carrot, and celery.

Again, most people measure by sight. The ingredients have to be covered by the liquid, and covered by enough liquid that they will remain covered even after the reduction in water as the stock cooks; on the other hand, there shouldn't be so much liquid that the stock will be bland. Knowing a ratio gives you the proper perspective and a benchmark from which to vary your own stock. A 3 : 2 ratio results in an excellent stock, with good flavor and body, and is an economical use of ingredients with a good yield. Good, given proper cooking temperature, appropriate aromatics, and handling relative to the type of stock. Fish bones are treated differently from veal bones, for instance. The following are recipes for the main stocks, and I've noted the nuances and specifics of handling each one.

## Stock Basics

Once you have the ratio and adjust it to your style and needs, the basics are clear.

Ingredients. Good fresh bones with plenty of connective tissue (tendons and joints are rich sources of gelatin, which gives stock body) and meat for flavor. Good fresh vegetables (carrot, onion, leek), fresh herbs, fresh spices such as peppercorns, collectively referred to as aromatics or aromats. Peppercorns don't impart a lot of flavor unless they're cracked, I've found. For optimal flavor, toast them briefly in a hot, dry pan and crack them with the bottom of a small sauté pan before adding them to your stock.

Beef and veal bones both benefit from blanching or roasting (bringing to a boil, then straining and rinsing in cold water; or cooking in a hot oven until they develop color and flavor). Both forms of heat set the exterior protein and get rid of some of the blood and protein that you don't want in your stock. Chicken bones can be started raw, but the stock should be skimmed as soon as the water is hot and the majority of the impurities have risen to the surface. Fish bones are often sweated, just until the protein is coagulated and the flesh and bone have become opaque, before the water is added. Vegetables also can be sweated, cooked until they begin to release moisture, but not cooked so much as to brown them. Vegetables can also be roasted or browned for a more complex and darker stock.

Temperature: always start your bones in cold water. In most cases, stocks should not boil, they shouldn't even simmer—180°F is optimal (a good method is to put the stockpot uncovered in an oven heated to below 200°F). This temperature extracts flavors without emulsifying fat and other impurities into the stock, clouding it and compromising its flavor, though it requires a little more time.

For stocks that must cook for more than an hour (vegetable and fish stocks do not), add the vegetables, herbs, and pepper at the end of the cooking so that they don't disintegrate and soak up your valuable stock when you strain them out. Add them during the last hour or so of cooking. Usually standard mirepoix will suffice: 2 parts onion, 1 part each carrot and celery. Celery can be omitted in a stock if you wish.

Tomato, often in the form of paste, is a unique and useful ingredient in that it adds acidity, sweetness, flavor, and an appealing brownish hue to stock.

When a stock is done, pass it through a strainer, then pass it through a cloth to collect as many particles as possible. Instead of cheesecloth, I buy inexpensive handkerchiefs, mark them indelibly, and use them exclusively for straining in the kitchen; they're more effective than most brands of cheesecloth, and they're washable.

Allow your stock to cool; refrigerate it uncovered until it's thoroughly chilled. Remove the layer of fat that will congeal on top, then store your stock, well covered, in the refrigerator or in the freezer. Gelatinous stock can be scooped into quart zip-top bags and refrigerated or frozen.

## Everyday Chicken Stock

When you have bones left over from roasting a bird, don't waste them—use them to make an easy basic stock. Stock from this simple recipe can be on hand if it's needed throughout the week. Stock making has the reputation of being a project, best reserved for a stretch when you have a lot of time, and requiring enormous pots, piles of raw materials, and long hours of tending, skimming, and straining. This kind of thinking does most of America a disservice. There is no reason why stock shouldn't be a part of every kitchen that would like to have it on hand.

> Bones from a roasted 3- to 4-pound chicken, along with any
>     meat still left on the carcass (or any baked chicken bones
>     totaling 1 to 1¼ pounds)
> 2 carrots
> 1 Spanish onion
> Kosher salt to taste
> Optional: a teaspoon of black peppercorns, a bay leaf, some
>     parsley sprigs, stems of thyme, a few cloves of garlic, leek tops,
>     a tablespoon of tomato paste—any or all of these items only
>     enhances the finished stock if, and only if, you happen to
>     have them available

Cut or pull the chicken carcass into pieces so that it fits in a 2-quart pot. Cover the bones with cold water. Put them over very low heat for 2 to 6 hours, just enough to keep the water heated to 180°F or 190°F (but not simmering). Add the remaining ingredients and cook for another hour over low heat. Strain into a clean pan or a 1-quart container.

YIELD: 1 QUART

NOTE: Because few of us roast a chicken for breakfast, and we won't want to finish making stock after dinner before bed, the bones can be stored in the refrigerator in a plastic bag until you're ready to use them (or frozen, for that matter, but that defeats the "everyday" nature of this stock). I usually start the stock the night I've roasted the chicken, as we're cleaning up, and turn it off after an hour or two and let it cool on the stovetop uncovered until I'm ready to finish it the following evening. The stock can be reheated then, the vegetables added, and the stock will be ready to strain in an hour.

### Traditional Chicken Stock

Chicken stock is valuable for its flavor, because it's economical to make and takes a relatively short time to prepare depending on the strength you prefer. It's an excellent cooking medium for legumes and grains and is a great base for countless soups. As with all stocks, one of the keys to its excellence is a gentle cooking temperature.

> 2 pounds raw chicken bones
> 3 pounds cold water (6 cups)
> ½ pound onions, chopped
> ¼ pound carrots, chopped
> ¼ pound celery, chopped
> 1 bay leaf
> 1 teaspoon peppercorns, crushed with the bottom of a sauté pan
> 2 to 3 stems of thyme
> 2 to 3 stems of parsley
> 2 to 3 cloves of garlic
> 2 tablespoons tomato paste

Cover the bones with the water in an appropriately sized pot (1.5-gallon stockpot is good). Put the pot over high heat and bring the water to a simmer. Skim the foam and congealed protein off the surface. Reduce the heat to low and cook for 4 hours (or place in an oven preheated to below 200°F; 180°F to 190°F is optimal). Add the remaining ingredients; they will cool the stock. Bring it back up to just below a simmer,

180°F or so, and continue to cook for another 45 minutes to an hour. Strain the stock, then pass it through a kitchen cloth.

YIELD: I QUART

## Veal Stock

Veal stock, brown and white—that is, stock made of roasted meat and bones (brown) and stock made of ingredients that have not been roasted (white)—is the most versatile and useful stock in the kitchen because of its abundant gelatin and neutral flavor: the meat and bones don't have a strong flavor of their own, and so magnify the flavors of what they're combined with. As they are the bones from a young animal, they contain abundant collagen, which breaks down into the gelatin that creates excellent body in the finished stock. Brown stock is the quintessential braising liquid—beef stews, osso buco, lamb shank, and short ribs are incomparable when cooked in veal stock. Veal stock adds depth and complexity to soups, and reduced by half, it becomes an instant sauce base, taking on the characteristics of whatever is added to it. The stuff is a wonder.

> *2 pounds meaty veal bones and veal joints, cut into 3-inch*
> *    pieces, blanched or roasted (see methods below)*
> *3 pounds cold water (6 cups)*
> *½ pound leeks*
> *½ pound onions, chopped*
> *½ pound carrots, chopped*
> *½ pound celery, chopped*
> *5 cloves garlic*
> *2 tablespoons tomato paste*
> *4 to 5 stems of thyme*
> *4 to 5 stems of parsley*
> *1 bay leaf*
> *1 teaspoon black peppercorns, crushed with the bottom of a*
> *    small sauté pan*

Combine the cooked bones and water in a pot and bring to a simmer. Reduce the heat so that the water stays just below a simmer, about 180°F, or place uncovered in an oven preheated to between 190°F and 200°F, and cook for about 10 hours. Add the remaining ingredients, bring the water temperature back up to just below simmering, and cook for 1 more hour. Strain out the bones and vegetables, and pass the stock through a kitchen cloth or cheesecloth.

See also the sidebar "The Remouillage" on page 97.

See also the sidebar "The Remouillage" on page 97.

YIELD: I QUART

### For White Veal Stock

*2 pounds meaty veal bones, cut into 2- or 3-inch pieces*
*3 pounds cold water for blanching*

Combine the bones and water in a large pot, bring the water up to a full boil over high heat. Strain the bones and rinse them well under cold water.

### For Brown Veal Stock

*3 pounds meaty veal bones, cut into 2- or 3-inch pieces*
*Vegetable oil*

Preheat your oven to 450°F. Lightly oil a roasting pan or a sheet tray large enough to contain the bones without crowding them.

Roast the veal bones in the oven, turning occasionally, until they are appealingly browned and smell delicious, about 45 minutes. They'll lose about a third of their weight, and the stock will be especially flavorful.

## Beef Stock

Beef stock can be handled the same way as veal stock with the same 3 : 2 proportions of water to bones, the same blanching or roasting of the bones, and the same adding of the vegetables during the last hour of cooking, though it's important that enough meat be included with the bones.

## The Remouillage

You can increase the yield of your veal stock by making a *remouillage,* which is simply a stock made by reusing the veal bones from your initial stock (*remouiller* is French for "to wet again"). Rinse the used bones in cold water, return them to a clean pot, and cover with cold water. The stock will be weaker, so it's best to use just enough water to completely cover the bones, but the flavor is nevertheless quite distinct and worth the trouble. Cook the *remouillage* for 6 to 8 hours. You can add fresh aromatic vegetables toward the end. Strain it as usual, and add it to your main veal stock. This can be used as is or it can be reduced to fortify it and strengthen the flavor.

If only bones are used, the stock will taste like bones, not beef, so at least a third of the weight should be meat; you may need to supplement your bones with additional beef (an inexpensive cut, the tougher the better, such as shank or round). I prefer a white beef stock (blanching the bones rather than roasting them), but they can be roasted if you wish.

### Fish Stock

Fish stock requires the freshest bones from white-fleshed fish—flounder, snapper, bass, sole, turbot. For the cleanest flavor, it's best to remove the heads, tails, veins, fins, and skin and to soak the bones in cold water in the refrigerator overnight to draw out any residual blood. For a basic fish stock, the 3 : 2 ratio works, though less water can be added. Aromatic vegetables are first sweated, then the bones are added to the vegetables and sweated, then the water and herbs are added, brought gently up to temperature. More than for any other stock, it's critical not to allow it to reach a boil. Fish stock requires less than an hour total cooking time.

## Fish Fumet

Fumet is a delicate, aromatic stock in which white wine has been included. For fumet, soak the bones overnight, use sweet white vegetables, such as onions, leeks, shallots, fennel, and mushrooms, if you wish, and use quite a bit less water, just enough to cover the ingredients.

*½ pound onions, thinly sliced*
*¼ pound fennel, thinly sliced*
*¼ pound leeks, thinly sliced*
*1 tablespoon canola oil*
*1 cup white wine*
*2 pounds fish bones (heads, tails, fins, and skin removed),*
*   soaked in water overnight*
*1 small bunch of parsley*
*1 small bunch of thyme*
*1 bay leaf*

Sweat the onions, fennel, and leeks in the oil over medium heat until soft but not brown. Add the white wine and continue to cook until the wine has cooked off (smell the pot; you should feel no alcoholic harshness in your nose). Add the fish bones and cook gently until they become opaque (cover the pot if you wish). Add enough cold water to cover the ingredients, add the remaining ingredients, and bring the stock slowly up to heat, lowering the heat just before it simmers. Cook for 30 minutes, remove from the heat, and let rest for 5 minutes. Strain as usual.

YIELD: ABOUT 3 CUPS

## Vegetable Stock

Vegetable stock should be sweet, mild, and aromatic. Any vegetables can be used, but stick to the sweet ones—onions, leeks, carrots—unless you have something specific in mind. Leeks are especially recommended for the body they give to vegetable stock. I don't recommend celery in vegetable broths because it tends to overpower the broth, and adds no sweetness and sometimes too much saltiness. Tomatoes give color, flavor, sweetness, and acidity to the stock; if you desire a light color, omit tomatoes. Mushrooms give vegetable stock a brothy, savory quality that it otherwise lacks. Sweating the vegetables first brings out their flavor in the broth; roasting them can make the stock more complex and interesting. The more finely chopped your vegetables, the faster they'll sweat and infuse the water. For a stock with stronger flavor, reduce the water by 25 percent, or you can reduce the finished stock to the desired strength. How you make the stock depends on how you want to use it. Is it a cooking medium for beans or a risotto, and therefore substantially reduced? Then you can make a lighter stock. If it is the base for a soup, you might want it stronger. Consider these factors when deciding how to shape your vegetable stock.

*½ pound onions, chopped*
*½ pound leeks, chopped*
*½ pound carrots, chopped*
*¼ pound fennel, chopped*
*¼ pound mushrooms (white or portobello with the gills scraped*
*    off), chopped*
*2 tablespoons tomato paste or 2 plum tomatoes, chopped*
*3 pounds cold water (6 cups)*
*1 small bunch of parsley*
*1 small bunch of thyme*
*1 bay leaf*
*Salt to taste (optional, depending on how you're using it)*

Combine all the ingredients except the salt and bring the water up to heat, just below a simmer, about 180°F, and cook for 1 hour. Add a small amount of salt, stir the stock, and taste—it should taste lightly seasoned, but you shouldn't taste the salt. Pass the stock through a strainer, then through cloth.

You may choose to sweat your vegetables in a couple of tablespoons of vegetable oil over medium heat, just until they soften and begin to release moisture, before adding the water, which enhances the stock's flavor. You may roast your vegetables in a moderately hot oven, or brown them in a hot pan, for a more complex sweetness and a deeper color. If you choose either of these, tomatoes can be added during the initial cooking or after the water has been added. Herbs and salt should be added after the water. Season with salt at the end of cooking.

YIELD: 1½ QUARTS

## Storing and Using Stock

Stock can be covered with plastic wrap or stored in a zip-top bag in the refrigerator for about a week or in the freezer for a month or more, depending on how well it's wrapped (eventually it will pick up odors).

When you have a good stock on hand, a great soup or sauce is moments away. And not just one, but countless ones. Obviously, one of the best things to do when you have stock is to feature it, use it in a preparation in which it's the main ingredient: soup. See page 103 for basic clear soup techniques and garnish suggestions. Here are a few more ways that stock can improve the quality of your life:

- Cook whole grains and legumes in a light stock (half stock, half water) or full-strength stock: brown rice, white rice, wheat berries, bulgur wheat, white beans, lentils, chickpeas.
- Twelve ounces of stock reduced by half becomes an excellent sauce base. Like soup, add some sweet aromatic vegetables such as minced shallot and herbs, and you have a wonderful sauce as is, or which can be further embellished with white wine or mustard and butter. Thicken it with a slurry or *beurre manié* (page 121).
- There is no better braising medium than stock. Again, an additional punch of sweet aromatics makes it all better. Sauté some onions and carrots with some salt in an ovenproof pan. In a separate pan, brown chicken legs or duck legs in hot oil. Add them to the sautéed vegetables, add enough stock to come two-thirds of the way up the chicken or duck, bring to a simmer, then place in a 300°F oven and cook for an hour or until tender. Place under a broiler to crisp the skin, and serve with the sauce and some hearty noodles. Add tomatoes or mushrooms to the braising liquid for more garnish.

- Use veal stock to braise short ribs or pot roast in the same way.
- Fish stock makes a wonderful base for bisque (thicken it as for cream soups, page 115). But fish stock also makes an extraordinary cooking medium. Tender fish can be shallow poached in a sauté pan for several minutes, removed from the pan, the heat turned on high to reduce the sauce, and adding some herbs, lemon juice, and some butter (or, for thickening, *beurre manié*, page 121).

The bottom line is this: it's not just that everything tastes better when you use fresh stock as opposed to factory-made broths, it's hard to make anything that's *not* delicious when you have good stock on hand.

# Clear Soups
# and the Consommé

Clear soups are among the easiest, most satisfying, and nutritious dishes you can make, period. If you have good stock. Good stock is critical. If you don't have a flavorful stock, you have to spend all your effort hiding the bad flavor of canned or boxed stock by adding all kinds of good ingredients. And why would you want to put good ingredients into a bad one? You might as well simply add those enhancements to water instead. The liquid is the flavor-delivery device, both of the actual ingredients and the garnish in the soup, as well as the infusion of aromatic goodness. Using canned broths to make soup is almost like serving really good food with bad-tasting silverware. Even something as simple as onion soup is better using plain water rather than canned stock. Stock isn't hard to make, it's just an additional step or cooking process. If you want to make soup, make the stock first (see Everyday Chicken Stock, page 93).

Once you have stock, soup takes about 5 seconds to make, with just about whatever you have on hand. Chopped tomatoes, corn, beans, pasta or rice, croutons (a great way to use day-old bread; toss with olive oil and toast), spinach or escarole, sausage or chunks of chicken, and fresh herbs are always fine. I love to put a raw egg in a hot bowl and pour piping hot soup into the bowl—the white will be cooked in a few minutes and the yolk will enrich the soup when you dig in. Season soup with salt and freshly ground black pepper, or perhaps some cayenne or Espelette pepper, or, depending on the garnish, some cumin and coriander or sriracha sauce or Thai curry paste or jerk seasoning or Parmigiano-Reggiano cheese.

Soups are simply stocks fortified with ingredients that you don't strain out. Begin by sautéing some sweet vegetables such as onions and carrots, about a cup if using a quart of the Everyday Chicken Stock (page 93), adding an aggressive 3-fingered pinch of salt, and cooking them until they're translucent. Add your stock. And add any additional garnish (noodles, vegetables, leftover chicken torn into bite-sized pieces) and you have a delicious soup but even plain, just with the onions and carrots, this is good to eat. When adding uncooked garnish to your soup, remember to add it so that each item will be perfectly cooked when you're ready to serve the soup; that is, if a soup includes both potato and a green, such as escarole or spinach, you would add the potato well before the greens, which cook in moments and can be added at the end. Soup is a great way to put leftovers to extraordinary use. Serve it with something crispy, such as a good baguette and some butter, and it's a satisfying meal.

Once you understand this, any number of variations are readily at hand if you follow standard or common flavor pairings. Begin all of the variations by sweating ½ cup of diced onion, ¼ cup of diced carrot, and if you wish, ¼ cup of diced celery for a quart of stock.

- *Corn-tortilla soup.* Add 2 cloves of minced garlic to the sweated onion mixture. Along with the stock, add a cup of corn and 2 diced Roma tomatoes, a cup of cooked and pulled or julienned chicken. Bring to a simmer, and taste for seasoning. Garnish with a diced avocado, a squeeze of lime, a pinch of cayenne or chipotle powder, julienned and fried corn tortillas, and torn cilantro leaves.
- *White bean, sausage, and escarole soup.* Sauté a pound of either loose or sliced link sausage (garlic sausage, page 134, is perfect for this, or add a few cloves of minced garlic along with the onions), add the onions and carrots and sauté until translucent; give the pot a 3-fingered pinch of salt as you do. If the sausage has released a lot of fat, pour this off. Add your stock and a cup of cooked white beans, bring up to heat, and season again with salt, pepper, and lemon juice as necessary. Stir in a large handful of julienned escarole and cook until wilted. Serve with a crisp baguette or a slice of ciabatta with salt and olive oil.

- *Curried yellow split pea soup.* Sauté onions and garlic and a couple of teaspoons of grated ginger until the onions are translucent, adding ½ teaspoon of salt as you cook them. Add a tablespoon of curry powder, a teaspoon of cumin, coriander, and turmeric, and ½ teaspoon of cayenne. Sauté until the spices are heated. Add your stock and a cup of yellow split peas and simmer until the peas are tender. Garnish with cilantro leaves and a squeeze of lemon. Serve with pappadams, the wonderful fried chickpea chips. This variation works well with lentils, too.
- *Vegetable soup.* Add minced garlic, about 2 cloves, once the onions and carrots are sweated, and cook this. Add a julienned leek, white part only, and sweat this. Add a quart of vegetable stock, then add ½ cup of diced turnip, diced celery root, seeded and chopped tomatoes, and the corn from 1 ear. Garnish with ½ teaspoon of picked thyme per bowl or torn parsley. Serve with crispy flat bread (see page 13).
- *Green curry soup with beef.* Sauté a tablespoon of green curry paste to cook it slightly, add the onions and carrots and sweat these, seasoning with salt. Add a pound of sliced or diced beef (use an inexpensive, well-marbled cut, such as a chuck roast trimmed of exterior fat) and sauté until it's no longer pink. Add 3 cups of beef stock, a cup of coconut milk, and a cup of peeled, diced potato. Cook gently until the potato is tender; garnish just before serving with sliced scallions and cilantro.

## Stock Perfected

But what to do if you are the sort who wants to take some of the very nice stock you've made and make it better, perfect it? To bring some of this finely made elixir, through some craftsmanship, to a state of crystal clarity and deep, rich flavor, to make the consummate stock? The cook then endeavors to make a consommé, one of the most satisfying dishes for a cook to prepare.

**Consommé = 12 parts stock : 3 parts meat : 1 part mirepoix : 1 part egg white**

A consommé is a perfectly clear soup, so clear that it looks like a distilled liquid. When you lift a spoonful, the bowl of the spoon should sparkle.

This liquid is so limpid, you are able, the saying goes, to read the date on a dime at the bottom of a gallon. It is stock perfected.

You don't see it offered often at restaurants because it takes some work and because it has a fussy reputation, the kind of thing you'd be served if you were lunching with an old wealthy relative you hadn't seen in years. And this is a shame because it's a pleasure to behold, to taste, and, most of all, to make. It gives true satisfaction to the cook.

The last restaurant I saw it prepared at was the Escoffier Room at the Culinary Institute of America, which teaches and serves classical French cuisine. The fellow, who serves as a kitchen manager and teacher's assistant, was Frank Jerbi, and he was the one responsible for making the consommé, twice a week for a year. He loved it. I tasted his and it was delicious. "What's the secret?" I asked.

"It's the ratio, man," he said. And he rattled it off: 5 quarts stock, 3 pounds meat, 1 pound mirepoix, 10 tomatoes, 10 egg whites.

The egg whites are what actually clarify the stock, forming as they coagulate with the meat into a kind of filter that traps the particles that make a stock cloudy. The filter, called "the clarification," or, after it's formed, "the raft," also traps flavor; thus the need to include meat and vegetables and herbs in the clarification. After the raft has formed, the stock is simmered gently to infuse it with more flavor and to further the clarification process. The broth is then ladled or gently strained through a coffee filter. And that is consommé.

I first learned how to make consommé at the CIA and this ratio is roughly based on what this school continues to teach, though I've reduced somewhat the amount of meat and increased the amount of egg white, so that the ratio would work best for smaller quantities.

### Consommé Using Any Stock

The consommé ratio (12 : 3 : 1 : 1) amounts to a 4 to 1 ratio of stock to meat, and 1 egg white for every 1½ cups of liquid. It should go without saying that for more flavor you can increase the quantity of meat and vegetables. Additional aromatics are also advisable—bay leaf, thyme, parsley, peppercorns, and even an oignon brûlée (an onion halved widthwise and deeply browned on the flat sides in a hot pan or on a griddle) for flavor and a deeper color.

> *48 ounces stock*
> *12 ounces ground lean meat*
> *4 ounces egg whites (3 or 4 egg whites)*
> *4 ounces mirepoix (2 ounces onion, 1 ounce carrot, and*
>   *1 ounce celery, chopped)*

Combine all the ingredients and bring them up to heat, being careful to stir with a flat-bottomed spoon continuously during the early cooking, dragging the spoon across the bottom and into the corners of the pot, in order to keep the egg whites from sticking to the bottom of the pan, where they will scorch. Reduce the heat as soon as it reaches a simmer and the raft has formed, just so that you have a gentle flow over and through the raft. Simmer gently for an hour.

Remove the pot from the heat. Lay a coffee filter in a strainer over the container that will hold your consommé. Ladle the soup into the coffee filter, trying to disturb the raft as little as possible. (A good strategy for larger batches of consommé is to siphon it out of the pot.) Skim any fat off the surface or drag some paper toweling over the surface to pick up any fat. Consommé can be chilled and reheated.

Garnish the soup with finely diced and blanched carrots, onions, leeks, celery, fresh herbs, slivered mushrooms, tortellini, diced custard, or other ingredients appropriate to the soup, though be careful of grains, which can cloud it.

YIELD: 1 QUART

## Chicken Consommé

Because chicken stock is the stock we typically have on hand at home, it's often the first choice of stock to use for consommé, and it's an excellent one. For the best flavored consommé, start with very rich, flavorful stock. One of the pleasures of the consommé is the way it shows off garnish, so take care to prepare the garnish well. For instance, take the time to make very small dice of the vegetables. Here I suggest shallots, carrots, celery, and shiitake mushrooms, but garnish could be anything from small-diced chicken to fresh herbs to lemon zest to orzo to Parmigiano-Reggiano. You can store consommé well covered for 2 to 3 days without compromising its flavor or clarity.

### FOR THE CONSOMMÉ

*4 ounces egg whites (3 or 4 egg whites), lightly whipped*
*4 ounces mirepoix (2 ounces onion, 1 ounce carrot, and*
  *1 ounce celery, chopped)*
*12 ounces chicken, preferably boneless, skinless thighs with fat*
  *removed, ground in a grinder or a food processor*
*48 ounces chicken stock*
*Optional: chopped plum tomatoes, thyme, parsley, black*
  *peppercorns (cracked), bay leaf*

### FOR THE GARNISH

*1½ tablespoons carrots, small dice*
*1½ tablespoons celery, small dice*
*4 shiitake mushrooms, julienned*
*1 tablespoon shallots, finely minced*

Combine all the consommé ingredients in a tall, narrow pot, preferably taller than it is wide (too wide a pot spreads out the clarification and allows too much reduction during cooking). Stir the ingredients to distribute the egg whites. Place the pot over high heat and stir with a flat-edged wooden spoon, dragging it along the bottom to prevent the egg whites from sticking and scorching. As the liquid gets hot, the protein will begin to coagulate and rise to the top. Continue to stir gently to make sure nothing is sticking to the bottom. As the liquid reaches a simmer, the solid ingredients will come together in a mass, a disk or raft. As this is forming, stop stirring and allow it to come together. Lower the heat before the stock boils, letting it get hot enough just to simmer over the raft and sink down through it. You should be able to see how clear the stock is at this point. Continue to simmer like this for 45 minutes to an hour. Don't let it boil, or the raft will disintegrate. After it's cooked, ladle the consommé through a strainer lined with a coffee filter. Your liquid should be perfectly clear. Taste. Add salt if necessary. Serve immediately in warm serving bowls, into which you've divided your garnish (see below), or chill the consommé in the refrigerator and cover with plastic wrap until you're ready to reheat and serve.

To prepare the garnish: Blanche the carrots and celery together in boiling water for 20 seconds, then strain under cold running water until thoroughly chilled.

Sauté the mushrooms in a small sauté pan in a teaspoon or so of oil over high heat, about a minute per side. Let them drain on paper towels. Cut them into fine julienne.

Combine the shallots, carrots, and celery.

YIELD: EIGHT 4-OUNCE PORTIONS

# THICKENING STOCK
# WITH STARCH: ROUX, SLURRY,
# *BEURRE MANIÉ*

S tocks are almost never an end in themselves, except when making a clear, fresh soup. Stock either becomes a cooking medium and the background of another dish, as with a risotto or dried beans, or its consistency and flavor are changed so that it can be featured in a dish, as with a cream or pureed soup or a sauce. A common and useful way of thickening stocks is with starch, either flour or a pure starch such as cornstarch, in one of three ways: using a roux (a cooked mixture of flour and fat), *beurre manié* (a raw mixture of flour and butter), or a slurry (a pure starch mixed with water). Each has distinct qualities and uses.

Starch granules thicken liquids by swelling and gelling as they're heated, absorbing water and releasing starch molecules into the liquid that create a mesh and prevent the water from moving around. In order for them to do this efficiently, the granules must be separated, either with fat (roux, *beurre manié*) or with water (slurry).

Once the particles are separated, the mixture is added to the liquid and brought up to temperature so that the starch can do

*Cream soups, such as this celery root soup, achieve ▶*
*an extraordinarily rich and voluptuous texture*
*when they're passed through a chinois.*

| 111

its thickening work. Roux requires some cooking and, after combining it with the stock, skimming for the best results. *Beurre manié* and slurries are typically *à la minute* methods of thickening, using them just before serving the dish. Slurries, especially those made with cornstarch, tend to break down more quickly than flour-based thickeners and so aren't used to thicken soups or sauces that must withstand repeated or extended heating.

# Roux

**Roux = 3 parts flour : 2 parts fat**

**Thickening Ratio = 10 parts liquid : 1 part roux**

Roux is flour cooked in butterfat and is an excellent thickening device for both soups and sauces. As the flour granules, which have been separated by a layer of fat and been partially cooked, heat up, they swell and release starch molecules, thickening the sauce. Thickening with roux is an underappreciated method of achieving a very fine consistency in a stock. While it has been associated with too-heavy classical French sauces, with the proper technique a roux-thickened sauce will be light and refined. If you've ever added flour to the cooking bacon and vegetables that begin a chowder, you've been making a roux. Roux not only changes texture, but it also adds some flavor and color, depend-ing on how long it's cooked. Roux can be cooked from pale (sometimes called blond) to dark brown, with deepening color and flavor. A roux is cooked when it begins to smell like a lightly cooked piecrust and is still pale, but it can be taken further, growing darker and more nutty in aroma. Two issues to be aware of regarding the color of roux are that if the roux cooks too much or too quickly, it can burn and become bitter, and that the more it's cooked, the less thickening power it will have. A roux cooked until it's nutty and brown has about half the thickening power of a pale roux.

The type of fat you use with the flour

matters. Classically, roux is made with flour and clarified butter. A roux can be made with vegetable oil, but it won't have a good flavor. If made with lard, it will. At home, and especially for small amounts, equal parts of flour and whole butter by weight can be used. You may want to cook some of the water out of the butter before adding the flour (butter includes about 15 percent water, which may start to break down the starch and thus reduce the roux-thickening strength).

The 3 : 2 ratio results in a roux of good consistency, not too thick and not too thin. Again, like stock, it's most convenient to measure by sight, melting your butter to cook off some of the water and adding flour in increments until you have the consistency of a paste.

To use roux, simply whisk it into the liquid; conventional wisdom advises that cold roux be mixed into hot liquid or the reverse in order to prevent the roux from clumping. (For more on using roux, see cream soups, page 116.)

The thickening ratio is for pale roux—roux cooked to a pale color, just enough to change the raw flour taste to one that's a little more cooked. If the roux is cooked to a dark, nutty brown, you may need to add as much as twice the amount to achieve the same consistency. Roux thickens fairly quickly, just as the liquid comes to a simmer. So you may choose to add your roux in increments until you have the consistency you want.

Plain stock thickened with roux is often referred to by its classical names, velouté (for white stocks) and brown sauce (for stocks made from roasted bones). These are two of the mother sauces of traditional French haute cuisine, as is béchamel (which is milk thickened with roux). They're typically made in restaurants, not at home, as soup or sauce bases, but it's helpful to know that if you make a clam chowder, you are in effect making a velouté.

A working recipe for velouté: Sweat 8 ounces of mirepoix, add 40 ounces of stock, raise the heat and bring the stock to a simmer, whisk in 4 ounces of roux, bring the mixture up to heat, pull the pot to the side of the heat, and skim as you cook it for 45 minutes to 1 hour, until the starchy flavor and feel is gone. Be sure to stir it often with a flat-edged wooden spoon to make sure the flour isn't sticking to the bottom and scorching. Strain through a chinois or a fine-mesh strainer. Finished velouté can be used as a base to make any number of derivative sauces simply by adding it to sautéed ingredients and finishing it with butter—mushrooms and cream for sauce supreme; shallot, wine, fish trim, and parsley for sauce Bercy—and to make soups.

Brown sauce is brown stock enhanced with browned mirepoix and thickened with roux, just like a velouté. Its main use has been in restaurants where it is served as a sauce base for dozens of classical sauces—bordelaise (red wine, shallots, herbs, lemon, bone marrow); chausseur (mushrooms, shallot, wine, brandy, tomato, herbs); or simply mushroom and shallot, finished with some butter. It's not used often in restaurants today; most chefs tend to work with natural reductions, but it remains a valuable technique, and anyone wanting to go through the trouble at home will be rewarded with a veal stock that requires no last-minute thickening—just add it to your cooked shallots and wine and herbs, add a little butter, and you're done. For a classical demi-glace, equal parts by volume of brown sauce and veal stock are cooked, skimmed, and reduced—this is, in effect, a much more flavorful version of brown sauce.

While velouté and brown sauce don't have a lot of uses in the home kitchen, their milk-based counterpart, béchamel, does. Béchamel is a base for cream soups, creamy sauces for pastas, *à la minute* sauces—such as a traditional cream sauce (finish with cream) or Nantua (finish with crayfish stock, brandy, cayenne, and butter)—and even such American classics as the boiled dressing for coleslaw and potato salad. It's rich without being overly fatty, easy to make, and inexpensive. Milk is your stock—can't get easier than that. I love the béchamel sauce. Again, the same ratio for thickening milk for a béchamel applies here as it does to a velouté, 10 parts milk, 1 part roux, meaning 10 ounces to 1 ounce, 24 ounces liquid to 2.4 ounces of roux, and so on, seasoned with aromatics, such as onions or shallots, and often some sweet spice such as nutmeg.

This will be used for the cream soups here, but it's a great base for creamy pasta with mushrooms, the base sauce for a lasagna, a traditional mac and cheese (finish it with plenty of grated cheddar or a Gruyère and Parmigiano-Reggiano), or the perfect biscuits with sausage gravy (see page 33 for biscuits, page 136 for breakfast sausage, and add plenty of cayenne to your béchamel).

## Cream Soups: Soups Thickened with Flour

The flour-thickened soups best known in American cuisine are gumbo and chowder. In France they have bisque, a shellfish stock once thickened with bread, now more commonly thickened with roux. But any manner of soup can be thickened with flour to create an extraordinary texture. Cream soups are a pleasure for their richness, flavor, and, especially, luxurious texture. They can be served cold in the summer and hot in the winter. While there are a number of methods for making a cream soup, using roux to thicken them is both efficient and healthy, because roux-thickened soups require considerably less fat than, say, cooking the vegetable in cream, without compromising a sense of richness.

A tablespoon of flour (cooked with a tablespoon of butter) will thicken 1 cup of liquid and this ratio can be used with any amount of stock or milk, depending on how much you want to make. Because roux is relatively inexpensive, it's good to make a little more than you need, to ensure that you're able to achieve the right consistency.

The general method is to thicken stock or milk with roux, cook the vegetable in it, puree it, check the soup's seasoning, strain it through a chinois, add the cream, and serve garnished with whole pieces of the vegetable. The chinois, a fine-mesh strainer, is the tool that will allow you to achieve that refined, luxurious texture. If you prefer a cream soup to have a coarser texture, a less fine-mesh strainer can be used or none at all.

As a rule, a cup of the chopped vegetable will flavor a cup of stock. You should use approximately 2 ounces of cooked vegetable as whole garnish per cup and use an ounce of cream per cup to finish the soup. So it's very easy to remember: 1 tablespoon of flour and butter, 1 cup of stock, 1 cup of vegetable, and 1 ounce of cream (often cream soups are finished with a liaison, cream to which egg yolk has been added, which enhances the liquid's texture). The following are general methods for cream soups that use chicken stock (mainly for green vegetables or chicken) or fish stock (for fish soups and chowders) and cream soups that use milk (mainly for root vegetables), with one example of each (broccoli and celery root).

An important step in using roux to thicken liquid is to cook the starchy flavor and feel out the sauce. This is done by pulling the pot off the center of the heat to create a convection current that deposits extraneous material from the flour and stock on the edge of the pot, where it can be skimmed away. Taste the liquid as it cooks, rub it against your palette—it should feel smooth, not grainy. This process takes 20 to 30 minutes. Also remember to stir the sauce regularly with a flat-edged wooden spoon to make sure the flour isn't sticking to the bottom of the pan and scorching.

For large quantities of sauce, roux is a good way of thickening—its impurities cook out of the sauce, it adds color and flavor that other methods don't, and it's less likely to congeal on the plate. But for thickening small quantities of sauce, *beurre manié* or slurry is recommended (page 121). At home, or in small quantities, roux is excellent for cream soups, bisques, and chowders.

### *Cream Soups Using Any Green Vegetable*

Green vegetable soups are easy, delicious, and nourishing if you have some good light stock on hand (see Everyday Chicken Stock, page 93). Classic soups made by this method are broccoli soup and asparagus soup, but snap peas and spinach also result in excellent soups. Season with lemon juice or white wine vinegar and garnish them with whole pieces of the vegetable, blanched, along with some crème fraîche for contrasting color and additional richness. The following recipe is excellent using broccoli, asparagus, English peas, snap peas (pods included), spinach, and celery.

> *1 ounce butter (2 tablespoons)*
> *1½ ounces flour (3 tablespoons)*
> *⅛ cup chopped onions*
> *Salt to taste*
> *3 cups chicken stock*
> *1 pound chopped vegetables, upper stems included, with about*
> *4 ounces reserved to use as garnish (florets of broccoli or tips*
> *of asparagus, for instance)*
> *Fresh lemon juice to taste*
> *3 ounces cream*
> *4 tablespoons crème fraîche (optional)*

Melt the butter over medium heat. Let it bubble to cook off some water (a half minute or so, but don't brown it), then add the flour and cook, stirring, for a couple of minutes, until the flour takes on a lightly cooked aroma. Add the onions, then a 3-fingered pinch of salt, and cook for another minute or two to sweat the onions. Add the stock and bring to a simmer, stirring and continually scraping the bottom so the flour doesn't stick and scorch. When the stock comes to a simmer, pull the pot to the edge of the burner and continue to simmer gently. Skim any foam or skin that collects on the cooler side of the pot. Add ¾ pound of the chopped vegetables and cook until tender, stirring occasionally to keep the flour from scorching on the bottom. Puree the soup in a blender on high for 2 to 3 minutes (cover the top of the blender with a towel and hold it down to prevent the hot liquid from splashing out), taste for seasoning, and add more salt if necessary. Add some lemon juice, 1 to 2 teaspoons, reblend, taste, and adjust as necessary. Strain the soup into a clean pan or serving dish, add the cream, and garnish with the reserved vegetables (see below), or chill immediately and reheat to serve.

To prepare the garnish: Bring a large pot of salted water to a boil (brine strength, see page 153). Cook the reserved vegetables as you like them, ideally slightly al dente. Strain and plunge them into ice water to halt their cooking. Drain on paper towels until ready to serve. This is called blanching and shocking.

YIELD: 4 SERVINGS

## Cream Soups Using Any Nongreen Vegetable

This is a great technique for making soups with many types of vegetables—beet, cauliflower, celery root, parsnip, potato, mushroom, sweet bell pepper. The soups are served hot in the winter and are enormously satisfying, but they can also be refreshing served cold in the summer. They give the impression of being very rich without using much cream. If you're serving them cold, you may want to season them with salt and lemon a little more aggressively. And, of course, they can be enhanced with any number of improvised seasoning variations (for instance, ginger in carrot soup, seasoning the mushroom soup with curry powder, garnishing the cauliflower soup with grated Parmigiano-Reggiano). Once you know the method, you can really begin to cook. Even if you're serving the soup hot, it can be made ahead of time, chilled, and reheated when you need it.

> *1 ounce flour (3 tablespoons)*
> *1½ ounces butter (3 tablespoons)*
> *⅓ cup chopped onions*
> *3 cups milk*
> *Salt to taste*
> *1 pound chopped vegetables; 4 ounces cooked until tender,*
>     *cooled, and reserved for garnish (see below)*
> *3 ounces cream*
> *Fresh lemon juice or white wine vinegar to taste*

Lightly cook the flour and butter over medium heat. Add the onions and cook for another minute or two. Add the milk and simmer until it's thickened, skimming any film that gathers on the surface. Salt to taste. Add the uncooked chopped vegetables to the béchamel and cook until they are tender. Puree the soup in a blender (cover the top of the blender with a towel and hold it down to prevent the hot liquid from splashing out), taste for seasoning, and add more salt if necessary, then strain it through a fine-mesh strainer into a clean pan or serving dish. Add the cream and season with lemon juice as necessary. Reheat the garnish in a microwave oven or in simmering water. Divide the garnish among the bowls, then pour in the soup.

For the vegetable garnish: Vegetable garnish can be cooked and cooled ahead of time, or while your soup is cooking as you would normally cook the vegetable. Most vegetables can be roasted or boiled, mushrooms and sweet bell peppers roasted or sautéed.

YIELD: 4 SERVINGS

# Beurre Manié and Slurry

**Beurre manié = 1 part flour : 1 part butter (by volume)**

**Slurry = 1 part cornstarch : 1 part water (by volume)**

**Thickening Rule = 1 tablespoon starch will thicken 1 cup liquid**

*Beurre manié,* or kneaded butter, is butter into which an equal volume of flour has been rubbed and kneaded, becoming an easy, effective way to thicken small amounts of sauces while also enriching them. Slurries, pure starch and water, may be quicker and more widely used, but they don't enrich or add flavor—butter does. *Beurre manié* is especially suited to thickening pan gravies, small quantities of *à la minute* sauces, meat stews, fish stews, and the poaching liquid in which fish has cooked. It should be used *à la minute,* just before serving.

A slurry is a mixture of a pure starch, such as cornstarch or arrowroot, and water. It's used to thicken sauces, a process often called lié (*jus de veau lié* is veal stock thickened with a slurry). Slurries are excellent for last-minute thickening, especially of sauces. The thickening will break down after repeated or extended cooking, so it's best to lié your sauce just before serving.

*Flour and butter in equal volume are kneaded ▶ together to form* beurre manié *("kneaded butter"), a paste that is whisked into sauces to both thicken and enrich them.*

You can use slurries to thicken larger quantities of liquid, such as soups, but this can create an unpleasant, overly gelatinized texture; roux is the recommended thickener for soups.

Most of the ratios in this book are measured in terms of parts by weight. This isn't practical when working with the small quantities here. In fact, making slurry and *beurre manié* is easiest to do using volume measures, and because we do most of our thickening by eye, the thickening rule simply provides the guideline that 1 tablespoon of any starch, whether flour or a pure starch such as cornstarch, will thicken to a light sauce consistency of 1 cup of liquid.

Here, the ratio is helpful for those who aren't familiar with slurries, but generally, it's best to mix a slurry by sight—it should have the viscosity and appearance of heavy cream—and add it to the hot liquid until you've reached the desired consistency. As a rule, though, 1 tablespoon of cornstarch mixed with enough water to separate the starch granules will thicken to medium consistency 1 cup of water.

I use *beurre manié* to thicken any sauce that benefits from a little butter. Which is pretty much any sauce! If you had a little fish stock and cooked a piece of fish in the stock in a small sauté pan, you could simply remove the fish, swirl in some *beurre manié* and have an elegant sauce to go with your fish (some fresh thyme or tarragon and a squeeze of lemon would go a long way here). If you have some veal stock (or beef), sauté some mushrooms and add them to the stock, bring to a simmer, and add a little *beurre manié* (a tablespoon per ½ cup of stock) and you will have a lovely sauce.

To demonstrate the effectiveness and versatility of *beurre manié,* I'm choosing one of the most common and wonderful preparations known: roast chicken. And to underscore the wonders of using water as a stock base, I've built the stock-making process into the method itself, which happens after the chicken is cooked, while it's resting.

Consistency is a critical factor in everything we eat. *Beurre manié* is one way we can regulate the consistency of liquids that add flavor and juiciness to our food. If you like it, make a cup or so by combining ½ cup of flour with a stick of soft butter, knead it to thoroughly distribute the flour, roll it in plastic wrap, and refrigerate until you need it. It will keep for a month refrigerated and for several months if frozen.

## *Roasted Chicken with Sauce* Fines Herbes: *A Lesson in Using Slurry or* Beurre Manié

Here is a very basic but also elegant way to roast and serve a chicken, simple and economical enough for a weekday meal, but elegant enough to serve the most honored guests. I honestly don't know if there's anything better in the kitchen than the whole process of roasting a chicken and preparing a sauce while it rests. A whole chicken this size takes an hour to roast, which gives you plenty of time to make accompaniments (mashed potatoes and buttery green beans sprinkled with salt and lemon juice are my favorites).

I especially like the sauce method here because it doesn't require chicken stock, only water (you will, in effect, be making your own quick stock right there in the pan you cooked the chicken in; though if you have some freshly made stock, perhaps from last week's chicken, see page 93, that's even better).

The main flavor of the sauce comes from the elegant mixture of herbs we call *fines herbes* (parsley, tarragon, chives, and chervil), dominated by the anise notes of tarragon and chervil. Don't worry about the chervil if it's not available to you, but then don't skimp on the tarragon. Unless, of course, you don't like tarragon! In that case, just use parsley and chives. You'll need about a tablespoon of finely chopped herbs to finish the sauce, but save a few complete stems to add to the sauce while you're cooking it.

The best way to roast a chicken this size is in very high heat, at least 450°F. If your oven isn't clean, this can result in a smoky kitchen if you don't have an exhaust hood, but I think it's worth it for the beautiful golden brown skin and the incomparably juicy chicken. It's important also to salt the chicken aggressively with kosher or coarse-grained salt. I prefer roasting the chicken in a medium cast-iron skillet or any oven-proof sauté pan just large enough to hold the bird. It's just the right size for making a pan sauce once the bird is roasted.

The sauce is made by quickly cooking the onion and carrot in the pan with the skin that has stuck to it, any neck or gizzard that you found in the bird, and the wing tips from the roasted chicken, first in wine until that is reduced and the pan is crackling and then water, developing great flavor by reducing the liquid all the way down. (When using wine, it's important that it's a wine you would happily drink, not so-called cooking wine.)

The sauce is strained into a small clean pan, reheated and thickened with a little *beurre manié,* and finished with the herbs.

> *1 roasting chicken (3 to 4 pounds)*
> *Kosher salt*
> *1 tablespoon butter kneaded with 1 tablespoon flour* or
>     *1 tablespoon cornstarch mixed with 1 tablespoon water*
> *1 tablespoon finely chopped parsley, tarragon, chervil, and*
>     *chives (one or any combination of these), with several stems*
>     *of each reserved*
> *1 medium yellow or white onion, thinly sliced*
> *1 large carrot, thinly sliced*
> *1 cup white wine*
> *2 teaspoons minced shallots*

Preheat your oven to 450°F (give it at least 25 minutes to get up to temperature).

Rinse and dry your bird, and keep the neck and any other innards except the liver (discard it or save it for another use). I like to truss the bird, pulling its legs together with butcher's string, crossing the two ends of the string and pulling them around the chicken, over the leg and wing, and tying the two ends at the neck; this results in a pretty cooked bird, one that rests more efficiently while you're making the sauce, with juicy white meat; while it's not strictly necessary, it's a definitively better roasted bird that comes out of the oven. A bird that's not trussed, as Bob del Grosso discovered while teaching at the CIA, can be as much as 10 percent lighter from water loss; trussing, he explains, closes up the body cavity, reducing airflow through it, and thereby reducing water loss. If you are not trussing the bird, I recommend stuffing the cavity with onion, a halved lemon, and any extra herbs you may have.

Salt the bird heavily with kosher salt; you'll need about a tablespoon in all; the bird should look almost as though it's got a crust of salt on it. Place the bird in an ovenproof skillet and pop it into the oven for

1 hour. (Prepare the accompaniments now and the remaining ingredients for the sauce.)

In a small bowl, combine the butter and flour, kneading it with your fingers until it becomes a uniform paste. Refrigerate it until you're ready to finish the sauce. Or combine the cornstarch and 1 tablespoon of water in a small bowl and set it near the stovetop.

Pick enough leaves of the parsley, tarragon, and chervil, if you're using it, and enough stems of chives so that you will have about a teaspoon of each once they're finely minced. Mince them and combine them. Reserve a few leafy stems of parsley and tarragon and a few stems of chives.

When the chicken has cooked for 1 hour, remove it from the oven. Stick a wooden spoon or other tool into the carcass to lift the bird out of the pan, allowing the skin to remain stuck to the pan. Set the bird on a cutting board or plate (it will release juices as it rests—you'll add these to the sauce). Place the pan over high heat to cook some of the juices down, and brown the skin that's stuck to the pan for a couple of minutes (be careful—the pan handle will remain very hot; keep a sturdy, dry kitchen towel over it). Remove the tips of the wings from the chicken and add them to the pan. Pour off all but 2 tablespoons of fat from the pan, return the pan to the heat, and add the onion and carrot and reserved herb stems; cook these for about a minute over high heat. Add the wine and boil the wine down, scraping the bottom of the pan with a flat-edged wooden spoon to get up all the skin and browned juices. When the wine is nearly gone, the pan will begin to crackle as the last of the wine cooks off. Stir the onion and carrot and chicken, cooking them more to brown them slightly. Add about a cup of water and repeat the reduction (use hot water to speed up the process a little). While this last reduction is happening, sweat the shallots in a film of canola oil or butter just to soften. When the water in the pan is gone and the pan is crackling, add 8 ounces of water along with the juices from the chicken (you can separate the legs from the carcass to get more juices), bring it to a boil for about a minute, and strain it into the saucepan with the shallots. Bring the sauce to a simmer and add the *beurre manié,* whisking or stirring until it is completely melted and the sauce has thickened. Remove it from the heat.

Remove each half of breast from the bird, keeping the wing attached (drawing your knife along either side of the breastbone, follow the wishbone down to the wing joint and cut through the joint). Remove the legs from the chicken and separate the legs and the thighs. Add the *fines herbes* to the sauce and rewarm as necessary. Serve with the chicken. Don't throw away the bones (see page 93)!

YIELD: SERVES 4

# PART THREE

# Meat:
# Sausage, Mousseline, and Other Meat-Related Ratios

# MEAT

I'd originally called this chapter *Farçir* because the French term accomplished so much. *Farçir* means "to stuff," and a *farce,* in professional kitchens, refers to a stuffing. In many kitchens and most cooking schools, the term for a meat stuffing has been Anglicized into *forcemeat,* probably the ugliest culinary term in the books. Forcemeat has gradually expanded to include any kind of meat, vegetable, or fish that's been seasoned and ground before being cooked, either inside some other food (a vegetable ravioli, for instance), in a casing (sausage), in a mold (*pâté en terrine*), or free-form (a pike quenelle).

But *farce* is confusing to the modern English-speaking cook, so I've taken it out of the title. That notwithstanding, the *farce* is an extraordinary cooking tool. It can bring you to the heights of pleasure, and yet it almost always uses common and inexpensive ingredients or provides a means for turning the trim from valuable ingredients into something shapely and delicious. *Farce* technique is ultimately one of economy and resourcefulness, and so it is the good cook who knows and understands the versatility of the technique.

While meat and vegetable stuffings are infinitely variable, depending on what you have on hand and the end result you're after, a few basic ratios are useful. The standard ratios taught in culinary schools involve

*Sausages, such as these made with scallops and ▶ shrimp, are among the glories of the craft of cooking.*

purees, namely the emulsified forcemeat and the mousseline forcemeat. I'll offer a basic ratio for sausage, because it makes the sausage easier, which is, of course, the beauty of the ratio. Sausage is ranked high on many people's lists of favorite things to eat, and I'd wager that the heartier the eater, the higher up it is, because the sausage may be unmatched in terms of deliciousness when it contains the right amount of fat and aggressive but judicial seasoning.

And the final ratio here is for a basic brine. Brines are used for several different ends and are another extraordinarily powerful tool in the kitchen that ought to be better and more frequently used by the home cook. They are used to cure food, preserve it, generate flavor, add their own flavor, and enhance succulence.

# The Noble Sausage

**Sausage = 3 parts meat : 1 part fat**

**Sausage Seasoning = 60 parts meat/fat : 1 part salt***

Sausage is one of the culinary glories when it's made and cooked right—a package of inexpensive trim, some fat, some seasoning that can be unparalleled in its deliciousness, in its ability to satisfy. A technique born of economy that results in the sublime. Truly, my respect for sausage knows no bounds.

Sausage can be made with just about anything you can fit into a casing (vegetables, rice, eggs, legumes, offal, blood), but sausage doesn't necessarily have to fit in a casing to be sausage—patties are part of the sausage tradition (relatives of the crepinette, which is a patty wrapped in caul fat) and free-form sausage is common as well in pasta, soups, and stews. Pot stickers

*To ensure juiciness, sausages should be between 25 ▶ and 30 percent fat. Sausage may be most familiar to us when stuffed into casing, as with this garlic sausage, but remember that sausage can be stuffed into pasta or dough or can be shaped and sliced or used loose.*

*Morton's kosher salt has a very close volume-to-weight correlation—½ ounce is 1 table-spoon by volume. The 60 : 1 ratio translates roughly to .25 ounce salt for every pound of meat and fat, or 1½ teaspoons for every pound of meat.

use a dough to enfold sausage. So, often, do raviolis. The above ratio concerns itself with traditional sausage, that is, sausage made with meat. Chicken, lamb, beef, pork, and venison all make wonderful sausages (fish does, too; see Mousseline, page 143). But the keys to a great sausage are first and foremost to blend the right proportion of meat to fat, and second to add the optimal proportion of salt to that meat-and-fat mixture. The advantage of the ratio here is that it can be scaled up or down as you need it. It's especially handy if you simply want to make a small portion, say 8 or 9 ounces (ground or chopped with ¾ teaspoon of salt and some garlic and herbs), to enhance a pasta or soup.

Without fat, sausages are dry and unpleasant. There is no such thing as a good, lean sausage. When chicken sausage tastes delicious, it's because it has the right amount of fat in it. (Be aware that store-bought chicken and turkey sausage are often made with what's called "mechanically separated" meat—meat and other fragments whipped off bird carcasses in a big spinner.) Commercial sausages that are both delicious and lean typically have some kind of chemical shenanigans going on in them to compensate for the lack of fat. Stick to natural foods, and you can eat fat and salt in comfortable proportions.

That is not to say that you can't use healthy techniques in your own sausages to reduce fat somewhat without compromising succulence. Vegetables and fruits can add moisture and flavor to sausages—roasted red peppers, onions, mushrooms, tomatoes, and apples make great additions to a sausage. Liquid fat, such as a flavorful olive oil, can be added to sausage, as can a wine or rich stock. But in the end, it's a fact we must embrace: the excellence in a sausage begins with the proper ratio of meat to fat.

That ratio is 3 to 1, 3 parts meat, 1 part fat. Ideally, 30 percent of a sausage is fat. This ratio amounts to 4 total parts with one of them, or 25 percent, being fat. The missing 5 percent is typically part of the meat that's being used—pork shoulder, for instance, or boneless chicken thighs, a great meat to transform into sausage. Indeed, some cuts are very lean; others are fatty, so some amount of eyeballing is required. Use your common sense. If you wanted to make a beef sausage with eye of round, venison, or other lean meats, you'd need a little bit more fat than the 1 part to 3 parts meat. Pork shoulder can come with the perfect proportion of fat already in it, so additional fat may not be needed when using pork shoulder. Thus, this ratio is one you almost always need to gauge with a scale and some common sense. If you're using very lean chicken, you'll need that full amount of fat. If you're using meat off beef short ribs, you won't need any.

The fat of choice is pork back fat, fat from the back of the hog—it's the fat that rims your pork chops but can be as much as 2 inches thick—it's very pure and supple and excellent for all *pâtés* and sausages. It can be ordered from your butcher or grocery-store meat department. And if it comes from a farm-raised pig, it's better for you than the more saturated fat from beef or lamb.

The next critical factor in creating the perfect sausage is salt. Sausages must have salt. Indeed, the word *sausage* derives from the Latin for salt. Originally, salt was the primary preservative element in sausage—it reduces bacteria activity—which was often dry cured and thus could be kept indefinitely. It remains so today in dry-cured sausages, but it is also the primary flavor enhancer in fresh sausages.

Never use iodized salt, which adds an acrid chemical flavor to food. Use kosher or sea salt only. Salt your meat well in advance of grinding it, so that the salt dissolves and penetrates (it will also help dissolve some of the meat protein, which will give the finished sausage a good bind and texture).

The ratio is .25 ounce of salt per pound of meat and fat, or about 1½ teaspoons of Morton's kosher salt. Because salt is so important to get right, it's best to weigh your salt—a tablespoon of fine sea salt, coarse sea salt, Morton's kosher, and Diamond Crystal kosher all have different weights. Morton's kosher is the closest to an even volume-to-weight ratio (a cup of Morton's weighs about 8 ounces); the volume measurements in the following sausages require Morton's kosher salt. If you're uncertain about the salt quantity you're adding, it's best to err on too little salt than too much.

There are a few important steps to making excellent sausage beyond the ingredients list. Sausage benefits from early seasoning. If possible, dice your meat and fat and toss it with the salt and seasonings the day before you grind it.

In terms of the actual making of the sausage, I've found there's one component that is more important than any other: keeping your meat cold at all times. This means if you're making sausage in a hot kitchen, it's prudent to partially freeze your meat before grinding it, and if you're not mixing it right away, keep it thoroughly chilled until you do.

After you've ground it, thoroughly mix it in the mixing bowl using a paddle to develop the protein myosin, which helps it all stick together. This also allows you an opportunity to add more flavor in the form of wine or olive oil (liquid also helps to distribute the seasonings and results in a juicier finished sausage).

The final element to the perfect sausage is cooking it right, taking it to the right temperature. The best way to gauge a sausage's temperature is with an instant-read or cable thermometer. Sausages are among the most abused foods when it comes to cooking them. They are almost always overcooked, and this can ruin a sausage. Pork sausages should be cooked to 150°F before being removed from the heat, and poultry-based sausages should be cooked to 160°F. If they are in a casing, they should be cooked in a way that browns them for flavor and texture, but remember, they cook best in moderate heat. Too much heat on a grill or in a blazing-hot pan will over-cook the outside before the inside is warm, and often will split the skin, releasing the juices and fat that make sausage taste good in the first place.

Apart from these critical steps the rest is seasoning, and this is up to the cook. When creating your own sausage, stick to pairings you know go well together. Chicken and tarragon or *fines herbes* go well—they would be excellent in a fresh chicken sausage. Dill is an herb you wouldn't normally pair with lamb. So if you were making a lamb sausage, you wouldn't combine it with dill; rosemary and garlic go well with lamb—so they'd also make great seasonings for a lamb sausage. Fresh black pepper and garlic alone is delicious. For rich meats such as venison, sweet spices go well. Fresh herbs are excellent in most sausages. For more exotic seasonings, you might look to other culinary traditions—Southwestern (cumin and dried chillis, roasted fresh peppers, cilantro) or Asian (scallions and ginger). Once you get the ratio right, there's no end to the kind of sausages you can create.

The following sausages are a few of the possible variations. Instructions assume you will be stuffing the meat into casings and twisting it into 6-inch links, but this is not strictly necessary. Loose sausage, sautéed in coarse chunks or as patties, tastes just as delicious. Loose sausage is great with all grains and legumes and pasta—everything from couscous to navy beans to barley to spaghetti.

## Spicy Garlic Sausage

Sometimes I wonder if God didn't create garlic specifically for sausage only to find out later that it went well with a lot of other things, too—because garlic and sausage are simply one of the great pairings. You almost don't need anything else, but I like one other element, either smoke or, here, heat. I make sausage in 5-pound batches, since that's the maximum that will fit in the 5- or 6-quart mixing bowl standard for most standing mixers; if you're going to make sausage, you might as well make a good amount. Sausage freezes well and will keep for a month or two in the freezer if well wrapped. Note that this is not a 3 : 1 ratio of meat to fat; because pork shoulder is fatty to begin with, there will be about 1⅓ pounds of total fat. Again, strive for fat that equals 30 percent of the total weight, 24 ounces in 5 pounds (80 ounces).

> *4 pounds boneless pork shoulder butt, diced*
> *1 pound pork fat, diced*
> *1.25 ounces kosher salt (about 2½ tablespoons)*
> *1 tablespoon freshly ground black pepper*
> *2 tablespoons dried red pepper flakes*
> *2 tablespoons minced garlic*
> *1 cup good red wine, ice cold*
> *10 feet hog casings, soaked in tepid water for at least*
>     *30 minutes and rinsed (optional)*

Toss the meat, fat, salt, black pepper, red pepper flakes, and garlic together until evenly mixed. Cover and refrigerate for 2 to 24 hours, until the mixture is thoroughly chilled. Alternately, place the mixture in your freezer for 30 minutes to an hour, until the meat is very cold, even stiff, but not frozen solid. Set the mixing bowl in a larger bowl of ice and grind the meat through a small die into the bowl.

Using the paddle attachment for a standing mixer (or a metal or strong wooden spoon if mixing by hand), mix on low speed or stir for 30 seconds; then add the wine and increase the mixing speed to medium and mix for 1 more minute or until the liquid is incorporated and the meat looks sticky.

Fry a bite-sized portion of the sausage and taste (refrigerate the sausage mixture while you do this and set up your stuffing equipment). Adjust the seasoning if necessary and repaddle to incorporate additional seasoning.

Stuff the sausage into the hog casings if using and cook to an internal temperature of 150°F, about 10 minutes in a sauté pan over medium-low heat or roasted in a 350°F oven.

YIELD: 5 POUNDS OF SAUSAGE, ABOUT TWENTY 6-INCH LINKS

## VARIATIONS ON SPICY GARLIC SAUSAGE

- *Hot Italian sausage.* Add 2 tablespoons fennel seeds, 3 tablespoons sweet paprika, and ¼ cup chopped fresh oregano to the spicy garlic sausage for traditional Italian sausage—use it loose with pasta and tomato sauce or make pasta dough (page 15) and use it to stuff raviolis.
- *Sweet Italian sausage.* Omit the chilli flakes and add 2 tablespoons sugar, 2 tablespoons fennel seeds, 3 tablespoons sweet paprika, and ¼ cup chopped fresh oregano.
- *Breakfast sausage.* Omit the chilli flakes; add ¼ cup each peeled and grated ginger and minced sage.
- *Duck or turkey sausage.* Replace the pork shoulder with diced duck or turkey (leg and thigh meat are preferable). Reduce the chilli flakes by half and add ½ cup minced sage.
- *Venison.* Venison makes an excellent sausage. When making venison sausage, discard the venison fat and use a full proportion of pork fat. Use half the chilli flakes and add ½ cup minced onion, ½ teaspoon each allspice and nutmeg, and 2 teaspoons each paprika and black pepper.
- *Mexican chorizo.* Omit the chilli flakes and add 1 tablespoon each ancho powder and chipotle powder, 1½ teaspoons cumin, and ½ cup chopped oregano.
- *All-beef sausage.* Replace the pork and fat in the spicy garlic sausage with meat and fat cut from beef short ribs; this can be stuffed into hog casings or, to forgo pork products altogether, into sheep casings.

- *Chicken sausage.* Replace the pork shoulder butt with boneless, skinless chicken thighs.

## Lamb Sausage with Olives and Citrus

Sausage can be made from just about any meat, and the way to create sausages of your own is to determine which meat that is and then use flavor pairings that you know work well. Here I combine lamb, olives (my favorite are Castelverano), and citrus, which is a great combination no matter the form of the meat. There's less salt added because the olives add their own salt. Because the salinity in olives varies, it's important to pay careful attention to the seasoning.

> *4 pounds lamb shoulder, diced*
> *1 pound pork fat, diced*
> *1 ounce salt (about 2 tablespoons Morton's kosher salt)*
> *Zest of 1 orange*
> *Zest of 1 lemon*
> *1 teaspoon black peppercorns, toasted and finely ground*
> *3 tablespoons coriander, toasted and finely ground*
> *¼ cup lemon juice*
> *½ cup orange juice*
> *¼ cup extra virgin olive oil*
> *¼ cup mint, minced*
> *1½ cups olives, chopped (use a variety of good, flavorful olives)*
> *10 feet hog casings, soaked in tepid water for at least*
> *    30 minutes and rinsed (optional)*

Combine the lamb, pork fat, salt, zests, black pepper, and coriander and toss well to distribute the seasonings. Cover and refrigerate for at least 2 hours or overnight.

Combine the lemon and orange juices and the olive oil and chill this mixture as well so that it is very cold when you use it.

Grind the lamb mixture through a small die into a bowl set in ice. Put the ground meat and mint in the bowl of a standing mixer with the chopped olives and mix on low for 30 to 60 seconds. Turn the mixer to medium-high and slowly add the juice-and-olive-oil mixture. Mix until it's well incorporated and the meat has an almost furry texture. Be sure to get some olives in the cooked portion you taste to check for seasoning, because they can bring a lot or a little salt, depending on how they were cured.

Stuff into the hog casings if using and twist into 6-inch links, shape into patties, or store as is to use loose. Cook for about 10 minutes in a sauté pan over medium-low heat or roast in a 350°F oven.

YIELD: 5 POUNDS OF SAUSAGE, ABOUT TWENTY 6-INCH LINKS

### Chicken Sausage with Basil and Roasted Red Peppers

I like to offer a chicken sausage for a couple of reasons. First and foremost is to prove that it can and should be every bit as decadent as a pork sausage and, second, that it can be even more flavorful than pork sausage. This is a variation of a sausage Brian Polcyn created for *Charcuterie,* but there's no reason you couldn't vary it in any direction you wanted—with the olive-citrus seasoning, as in the lamb sausage recipe above, or with garlic and pepper, or *fines herbes.* A chicken sausage, made with readily available boneless thighs, is a great vehicle for flavor.

*3½ pounds boneless, skinless chicken thighs, cubed*
*1½ pounds pork fat, cubed*
*1.25 ounces kosher salt (about 2½ tablespoons)*
*1 teaspoon freshly ground black pepper*
*1 tablespoon garlic, minced*
*½ cup tightly packed basil, chopped*
*½ cup diced roasted red pepper (1 or 2 red peppers, charred,*
   *peeled, and seeded)*
*¼ cup red wine vinegar, chilled*
*¼ cup extra virgin olive oil*
*¼ cup dry red wine, chilled*
*10 feet hog casings, soaked in tepid water for at least*
   *30 minutes and rinsed (optional)*

Toss the chicken, fat, salt, pepper, garlic, basil, and red pepper together until evenly mixed. Grind the mixture through a small die into a bowl set in ice.

Using the paddle attachment for a standing mixer (or a metal or strong wooden spoon if mixing by hand), paddle on low speed or stir for 1 minute; then add the vinegar, oil, and wine and increase the mixing speed to medium and mix for 1 more minute or until the liquid is incorporated.

Fry a bite-sized portion of the sausage, taste, and adjust the seasoning if necessary.

Stuff the sausage into the hog casings if using and twist into 6-inch links. Sauté, roast, or grill over medium-low heat to an internal temperature of 160°F.

YIELD: 5 POUNDS OF SAUSAGE, ABOUT TWENTY 6-INCH LINKS

## Fresh Bratwurst

There are as many forms of bratwurst in Germany as there are salamis in Italy. The brats I've come to love in the United States are dominated by sweet spices such as nutmeg. I'm also adding some marjoram, which is common in the Silesia region of Germany, to this recipe, because marjoram is an underused herb and it's a favorite of my partner in charcuterie, Brian Polcyn, who taught me the finesse elements of making sausage.

*4 pounds pork shoulder, diced*
*1 pound pork backfat, diced*
*1.25 ounces kosher salt (about 2½ tablespoons)*
*2 teaspoons freshly ground black pepper*
*1 tablespoon ground nutmeg*
*1 tablespoon ground ginger*
*¼ cup chopped marjoram*
*½ cup white wine, chilled*
*10 feet hog casings, soaked in tepid water for at least*
   *30 minutes and rinsed (optional)*

Toss the meat, fat, salt, pepper, nutmeg, ginger, and marjoram together until evenly mixed. Cover and refrigerate for 2 to 24 hours, until the mixture is thoroughly chilled. Alternately, place in your freezer for 30 minutes to an hour, until the meat is very cold, even stiff, but not frozen solid.

Grind the mixture through a small die into the mixing bowl of a standing mixer set in a bowl of ice.

Using the paddle attachment for a standing mixer (or a metal or strong wooden spoon if mixing by hand), mix on low speed or stir for 30 seconds; then add the wine and increase the mixing speed to medium and mix for 1 more minute or until the liquid is incorporated and the meat looks sticky.

Fry a bite-sized portion of the sausage and taste (refrigerate the sausage mixture while you do this and set up your stuffing equipment). Adjust the seasoning if necessary and repaddle to incorporate additional seasoning.

Stuff the sausage into the hog casings if using and twist into 6-inch links. Cook to an internal temperature of 150°F, about 10 minutes in a sauté pan over medium-low heat or roasted in a 350°F oven.

YIELD: 5 POUNDS OF SAUSAGE, ABOUT TWENTY 6-INCH LINKS

## Beyond the Noble Sausage

Once you know the meat-fat ratio and the salt-per-pound ratio, you can transform any meat into sausage, but that doesn't mean you should stop there. There are endless preparations that use ground meat that we don't think of as sausage. Pot stickers are filled with what is, in effect, sausage— a ground meat stuffing, or *farce*. Meat loaf is nothing more than a free-form sausage. A *pâté en terrine* is a basic sausage with lots of extra seasoning and aromatics and interior garnish—mushrooms and herbs and pistachios—spread in a terrine mold, covered, and baked in a water bath like a custard to a temperature of 150°F (or 160°F if using chicken). Meatballs are a form of sausage. I'm not going to say that hamburgers are sausage, but, well, they are the same idea. In fact, it's a great practice to season your hamburger meat a day ahead of cooking it: follow the .25

ounce of kosher salt per pound, and you will have perfectly seasoned burgers.

## VARIATIONS BEYOND SAUSAGE

- Make extraordinary pot stickers by adding minced garlic, ginger, and scallion to a basic pork sausage (a dough can be made by mixing 1 part cold water into 2 parts flour—3 ounces water and a cup of flour—until a dough is formed; or you can use wonton wrappers if you wish). Fry the pot stickers in a film of oil, then add a couple of cups of Everyday Chicken Stock (page 93), cover, and simmer until done, about 15 minutes.
- *Stuffed peppers.* Peppers were practically designed to carry sausage. Fill them with any kind of sausage and grill (or roast) them until the sausage is done (150°F; 160°F for chicken sausage). It's best to use banana peppers or ones that don't require a boatload of sausage. You want a good ratio of pepper to sausage). Another option is to scoop the seeds out of a halved zucchini, stuff that with sausage, and grill (or roast).
- *Make meatballs.* To a basic grind of beef with 25–30 percent fat, add .25 ounce of salt per pound; ½ cup of diced onion sautéed with a couple of cloves of minced garlic; a couple of pieces of day-old bread, chopped, soaked in milk, and squeezed out; an egg; and ¼ cup of chopped oregano, if you wish. The key to good meatballs, unlike a sausage, which is thoroughly mixed, is not to overmix it. Gently combine the ingredients, just so they are evenly distributed and form into balls. Flour them and panfry.

  Make the meatball mixture using a combination of beef, veal, and pork, form into a loaf, and bake at 350°F to an internal temperature of 155°F, for *meat loaf.*
- *Keftedes, a version of Greek meatballs.* Working with Cleveland chef and friend Michael Symon, I learned his preference for meatballs, which he serves either as a main course or as an hors d'oeuvre—seasoning beef or lamb with black pepper, coriander, garlic, and lemon zest. He serves them panfried with lemon zest, torn fresh herbs, mint, cilantro, and some crumbled feta cheese.

- *Stuffed flank steak.* Use the keftedes or meatball mixture to roll inside a flank steak, tie the steak, and braise in a loaf pan in veal stock (page 95) until the beef is fork tender. Skim the fat from the sauce and reduce the sauce, whisking in a tablespoon or two of butter (or *beurre manié,* page 121) just before removing it from the heat, and serve with the sliced meat.

# Mousseline

## Mousseline = 8 parts meat : 4 parts cream : 1 part egg

A mousseline *farce* is a delicate emulsion of meat, cream, and egg used to create finely textured sausages, terrines, quenelles, and stuffings. It's perhaps the easiest kind of *farce* to make at home because the ingredients are common, the only equipment needed is a food processor, and mousseline is very stable, meaning the fat (cream) and meat won't easily separate, or break.

Varying the amount of cream will affect the flavor and texture—as much as 50 percent more cream is common and results in a lighter texture and a milder flavor (you'll need to season it a little more aggressively). And it does not have to be plain cream—you might choose something with a more distinct flavor, such as sour cream, mascarpone, or thick yogurt. Or if you don't have cream on hand, very soft butter is a good substitute here. Also, you might infuse your cream with flavor (basil or saffron, for instance).

As for the egg, a yolk adds some richness but is by no means necessary. Many if not the majority of mousselines don't use yolks at all, and yolks must be left out if you want the *farce* to remain very white. An

*Mousseline, such as this chicken with* fines herbes, ▶ *is a kind of sausage or* farce—*pureed meat and cream, egg, and seasoning—that has myriad uses. It can be shaped into quenelles and poached, stuffed into casing, or used to fill a ravioli or a dumpling.*

alternate volume ratio that works just as well and that is fairly standard in culinary textbooks is this: mousseline = 1 pound meat : 1 cup cream : 1 egg.

And yet even the egg is expendable—though you would never puree meat straight and cook it (without enough fat, it would be rubbery)— what you use to lighten, soften, and bind it doesn't have to include egg. Corey Lee, chef de cuisine at the French Laundry, makes a chicken *farce* that uses crème fraîche and chicken stock but no egg. So the preparation is very flexible.

The only critical points of the technique are, first, all ingredients should be very, very cold (as close to freezing without being frozen is optimal), and, second, the cream should be added gradually (as with emulsified sauces such as mayonnaise and hollandaise). So it's as simple as putting the egg and meat in a food processor, turning it on, and pouring in the cream in a thin stream. (For very refined preparations you may want to press fish mousselines through a tamis, or drum sieve, to remove any fine connective tissue that may not have been pureed.)

The mousseline forcemeat is not only simple, it's incredibly versatile and, frankly, fun. It makes cool sausages, especially if you fold in chunks of garnish—a shrimp mousseline with chunks of lobster and diced leek, for instance, for a seafood sausage. *Pâtés en terrine* are a snap. Quenelles can be dropped like dumplings into soup. A chicken breast filled with some chicken mousseline (into which you've stirred some sautéed mushrooms, or better, some chopped black truffles)—well, it's not a chicken breast anymore, it's something a whole lot better.

### Basic Mousseline Forcemeat

*8 ounces lean white meat or fish, diced*
*1 large egg (or 2 large egg whites)*
*½ teaspoon salt*
*4 ounces cream*

Make sure all the ingredients have been well chilled in the refrigerator (or even placed in the freezer for 15 to 20 minutes). Put the meat or fish, egg (or egg whites), and salt in a food processor and pulse to puree the meat and combine the ingredients.

With the machine running, pour the cream, in a thin stream, into the processor. When all the cream has been incorporated, drop a teaspoonful into 180°F water and cook through, 5 to 10 minutes, and taste for seasoning. Adjust the seasoning if necessary and keep the mousseline refrigerated until ready to use. If shaping into a roulade, poach it for 30 to 40 minutes to a temperature of 145°F for fish and 160°F for poultry. It can be held well wrapped and refrigerated for a day.

## Ways to Use a Basic Mousseline

This mousseline can be made with just about any protein, but traditionally it's made with white meat. This method is best used with shrimp, scallops, salmon, pike, and trout, as well as veal, chicken, partridge, and other game birds. Friend, chef, and instructor Dan Hugelier offers a red meat exception, though: oxtail mousseline used to make a ravioli (but, Dan adds, "the addition of foie gras, sweetbreads, and other ingredients would enhance it").

Mousselines can be used to stuff pasta or other doughs for dumplings and raviolis (shrimp mousseline puffs, so don't pack it tight). They can be baked in molds (a classical application straight out of Escoffier, before they had food processors and had to pound the fish and press it through a tamis). Chunky garnish may be folded into them (chunks of shrimp or clams in scallop mousseline can be dropped by the spoonful into a seafood broth). Mousseline can be thought of simply as a delicious binder—infuse the cream for your mousseline with saffron and mix abundant crab into it to make exquisite crab cakes. A veal mousseline might enfold chunks of sautéed mushrooms to be piped into a pocket cut into a chicken breast.

Or make an easy salmon terrine: You'll need a pound of salmon, plus one ½-pound center-cut fillet to use whole as a garnish. Cut the center-cut fillet into a 1½- by 1½-inch strip or strips the length of your mold, season with salt, and reserve. Add any trim from this piece to your diced salmon. Make double the basic mousseline (page 144), using the pound of diced salmon along with any trim, and adding a tablespoon each of lemon zest, orange zest, and minced chives to the salmon before pureeing with the eggs and adding the cream. Line your terrine mold with plastic wrap, with enough overhang to cover the mold when it's full. Spread half the mixture in the terrine mold. Lay the strip or strips of salmon along the center of the mold, and cover with the remaining mousseline. Fold the plastic wrap over the top of the terrine. Cover the terrine with foil, and bake in a water bath at 300°F, as with a custard (page 199), to an internal temperature of 140°F. Chill completely, unmold, pat dry, and slice to serve with some crème fraîche and a chiffonade of basil or with some Lemon-Shallot Mayonnaise (page 172).

Salmon terrine with shrimp and basil, a variation on the above salmon terrine. Make double the basic mousseline (page 144) using a pound of diced salmon. Fold into the mixture ½ cup of julienned basil. Spread half the mixture in a terrine mold; lay large shrimp on their sides, interlocking, along the length of the terrine. Spread the remaining mixture on the shrimp. Cook and chill as with the above terrine.

## Shrimp Dumplings

Shrimp makes a very stable, flavorful stuffing when pureed in the style of a mousseline, one of the most versatile in the kitchen. It can be used to make raviolis, shrimp toast (see the variation on page 147), quenelles, or sausages (see the following recipe). This recipe uses the basic mousseline proportions exactly, with the addition of some aromatics—scallions, ginger, and garlic.

> 8 ounces shrimp, peeled (shells reserved for stock if you wish; see
>   page 147)
> 1 large egg (or 2 large egg whites)
> ½ teaspoon salt
> 1 teaspoon peeled and grated ginger
> 1 teaspoon minced garlic
> 2 scallions, coarsely chopped
> 4 ounces cream
> 20 wonton wrappers
> Egg wash: 1 large egg mixed with 2 tablespoons water

Combine the shrimp, egg, salt, ginger, garlic, and scallions in the bowl of a food processor (the shrimp should be as cold as possible). Pulse the blade a few times, then, with the motor running, add the cream in a thin, steady stream.

Spoon a tablespoon or so of the mixture into the center of each won-ton wrapper, brush half the dough with egg wash, and fold the dough closed in a half-moon shape.

Sauté the dumplings in oil until browned, add shrimp or chicken stock (see below or page 93), bring to a simmer, cover, and finish cooking. Serve in the broth or with a dipping sauce (see tempura batter, page 78).

To make a quick shrimp stock, sauté the shells with a sliced shallot, a teaspoon of tomato paste, and a healthy pinch of salt until they're cooked and colored; add water just to cover, and simmer gently for 15 minutes. If you have access to lemongrass, this can be added as well. Strain through a metal strainer, crushing the shells to extract as much liquid as possible, then strain through cloth.

Variation: *Shrimp toast.* Spread the mousseline on thinly sliced white bread (from a Pullman loaf or any loaf from which you might make toast points, such as Pepperidge Farm sandwich bread). Cut in quarters diag-onally or as you wish, sprinkle with sesame seeds, and shallow fry. Serve with a simple soy dipping sauce (see page 79).

## *Shrimp and Scallop Sausage*

Mousseline forcemeats are the easiest and most stable to make at home and quickly come together in a food processor. This elegant *farce* can be stuffed into sheep casing or hog casing or shaped into quenelles and used in clear seafood broths.

This recipe calls for half the standard ratio of cream because scallops have less structure generally than other meat (such as shrimp or chicken). Also, depending on your source, they can be waterlogged and throw off the recipe; try to buy "dry-packed" scallops. But they result in a very delicate and delicately flavored *farce* that works well as a sausage and can be served on its own, with a lemon *beurre blanc,* for instance, or Lemon-Shallot Mayonnaise (page 172). This recipe can also be reversed—you might make a shrimp mousseline (straightforward ratio, 1 pound shrimp, 1 egg or 2 egg whites, and 1 cup of cream) and fold in chunks of scallops.

*1 pound scallops*

*2 large egg whites*

*1 teaspoon kosher salt*

*½ cup cream*

*1 leek, white part only, thoroughly cleaned, small diced, and
sautéed in butter until tender, then chilled*

*8 ounces shrimp, peeled, deveined, and roughly chopped*

*1 tablespoon chives, chopped*

*4 feet sheep casing or 3 feet hog casing, soaked in tepid water
for at least 30 minutes and rinsed (optional)*

Puree the scallops with the egg whites and salt in a food processor. Check the consistency. Some scallops are waterlogged. With the machine running, slowly add half the cream. If it's very loose, you may not need all the cream. The mixture should be stiff enough to shape. Continue adding the rest of the cream with the machine running if the *farce* remains stiff.

In a mixing bowl combine the *farce* with the leek, shrimp, and chives, gently folding the garnish to distribute it evenly.

Stuff into the sheep casing if using. Sauté in a little butter or vegetable oil over medium heat to an internal temperature of 140°F and serve, or poach in 170°F stock or water to an internal temperature of 135°F, and chill in an ice bath, then gently sauté to reheat and serve. Alternately, you can form into a roulade using plastic wrap, tie off each end, and poach in water. Chill and serve sliced cold with Lemon-Shallot Mayonnaise (page 172) or sauté to reheat.

## Agnolotti with an Herbed Chicken Stuffing

Agnolotti are crescent-shaped ravioli, but these agnolotti are an ingenious self-sealing ravioli I learned from the French Laundry. They work well with just about any stuffing you can pipe, from thick vegetable purees to starches to meat-based stuffings such as this chicken mousseline (or any sausage recipe, provided it's well pureed—such as the above scallop mousseline). The agnolotti technique is excellent for making a lot of ravioli quickly; the method also prevents air pockets, and all the folds in the dough help them carry liquids and sauce. If you want to forgo the pasta, though, this mousseline can be scraped between two spoons to form quenelles and dropped into a chicken soup. Adding quenelles is a way to make an everyday soup elegant. The mousseline can be made up to a day in advance.

> *½ pound boneless, skinless chicken thighs, diced and well chilled*
> *1 large egg*
> *½ teaspoon salt*
> *½ cup cream*
> *1 teaspoon each tarragon, parsley, and chive, chopped*
> *¼ teaspoon black pepper*
> *⅛ teaspoon cayenne*
> *1 recipe Basic Pasta Dough (page 17)*
> *Egg wash: 1 large egg mixed with 2 tablespoons water*

Combine the chicken-thigh meat, egg, and salt in the bowl of a food processor. Combine the cream, herbs, pepper, and cayenne and, with the processor running, add the cream in a thin, steady stream. Refrigerate the mousseline until ready to cook or make the agnolotti.

To make the agnolotti, roll the pasta out through the thinnest roller setting. Do this one setting at a time so that the dough remains supple. Make sure you roll the sheets so that they are at least 4 inches wide and about 18 inches long. Put the mousseline in a pastry bag fitted with a ½-inch tip. Pipe the mousseline along the length of one sheet, just off center. Brush the pasta on one side of the piped mousseline with egg wash to ensure a good seal. Fold the pasta over the mousseline and tuck it snugly around the *farce*. Press off the agnolotti in 1-inch increments, making sure there's a good seal between them. Using a fluted pastry wheel (or knife), cut a clean edge along the length of the pasta, then cut each agnolotti. Transfer to a plate or tray dusted with flour (semolina or cornmeal works best to prevent sticking), cover, and refrigerate until ready to cook. These can also be frozen and used later.

YIELD: SERVES 4

VARIATIONS

- Use these dumplings in a clear leek and mushroom soup with chicken agnolotti, using a quart of Everyday Chicken Stock (page 93) and sautéed leeks and mushrooms for garnish (see clear soups, page 103).
- Boil them until the pasta is tender and the chicken cooked through, 5 minutes or so, and serve with a basic tomato sauce and mozzarella cheese, garnished with chopped parsley and lemon zest.
- Replace the *fines herbes* with ½ cup of chopped basil and the zest from 2 lemons.
- Replace the *fines herbes* with chopped mushrooms that have been sautéed with minced shallots, then fully chilled.
- For a vegetarian agnolotti, a ricotta *farce* can replace the chicken mousseline: Combine in a bowl 1 cup ricotta (drained if it's very moist), ½ cup grated Parmigiano-Reggiano, a teaspoon of lemon juice and lime juice, the zest from the lemon and lime, 2 tablespoons chopped chives, 2 tablespoons minced parsley, ¼ teaspoon salt, and ⅛ teaspoon cayenne powder, and mix until the ingredients are uniformly distributed. Taste for seasoning and adjust it if necessary.

## Boudin Blanc

Boudin Blanc is a very easy sausage to make and is flavored predominantly with *quatre épices*, the traditional *pâté* seasoning of pepper, cinnamon, cloves, and nutmeg (3 : 1 : 1 : 1 by volume). This is a tradition in France at Christmastime. I've added diced shiitake mushrooms to the traditional mousseline. They're excellent served with mashed potatoes and some spiced poached fruit.

> *1 pound pork shoulder butt, cut into 1-inch dice*
> *1 pound boneless, skinless chicken thighs, cut into 1-inch dice*
> *1 ounce kosher salt (about 2 tablespoons)*

*1½ teaspoons* quatre épices *(recipe follows)*
*8 large eggs*
*2½ cups milk*
*3 tablespoons flour*
*8 feet hog casings, soaked in tepid water for at least 30 minutes
    and rinsed (optional)*

Grind the meats together into a bowl set in ice. Place the meat in the freezer for 5 minutes and prepare the food processor.

Combine the ground meat, salt, and *quatre épices* in the processor and puree to combine, about 30 seconds. With the processor running, add the eggs one or two at a time, followed by the milk, then the flour. You may need to stop to scrape down the sides of the bowl.

Do a "quenelle test" to check for seasoning: wrap a heaping tablespoon in plastic and poach it in 180°F water until it reaches 160°F, about 10 minutes. Keep the rest refrigerated while you cook the quenelle. Taste the quenelle and adjust the seasoning if necessary, repaddling only long enough to distribute the new seasoning.

Stuff into the hog casings if using and poach in 175°F water to an internal temperature of 160°F. Shock in ice water until chilled.

Brown in butter over medium heat and serve.

YIELD: 4 POUNDS OF SAUSAGE, ABOUT SIXTEEN 6-INCH LINKS

## Quatre Épices

*1 teaspoon black pepper*
*⅛ teaspoon ground cinnamon*
*⅛ teaspoon ground cloves*
*⅛ teaspoon ground nutmeg*

Combine and store in an airtight container.

YIELD: 2 TEASPOONS

# Brine

## Brine = 20 parts water : 1 part salt

Brine, salt in solution, is an astonishingly powerful tool. It will season the interior of pork loin and keep that loin extremely juicy; it will cure a beef brisket or a ham; it will facilitate the transformation of raw vegetables into tangy delicious pickles; it will protect virtually any food from decay. Such is the miracle of salt. But because salt is so powerful, it can easily be misused. Oversalting food can make it impossible to eat in a way that, say, overcooking food rarely does. So it's always better to undersalt than to oversalt food. But, the mark of a talented cook, indeed what professional cooks are taught first, is the ability to salt food exactly right. We need salt to live, thus our bodies have become very good at tasting and regulating it (we're less good at regulating it when it's hidden in our food, such as in canned soups, processed snacks, and fast food).

Turning salt into liquid makes it an especially effective tool because it touches 100 percent of the food's surface in a uniform concentration. Salt has to dissolve before it can work its magic, so using dry salt is less

*Brines—salt and seasonings in liquid—is one of ▶ the most powerful tools in the kitchen, flavoring, or preserving all manner of fruits, vegetables, and meats. The brine seasoning used to corn beef includes the sweet and spicy ingredients pictured here: cinnamon and allspice, nutmeg and brown sugar, coriander and chilli flakes, garlic and black pepper.*

quick, less controlled, than using a brine. Brine concentration is critical. If it's too strong, it can overpower the food it surrounds. While food that becomes too salty from a brine can be fixed simply by soaking it in water until the salt has returned to the water, it's far better to make the right concentration of brine to begin with, and to submerge the food for the appropriate time.

The ideal brine is 5 percent salt (or 20 parts water, 1 part salt) by weight. That means 20 ounces of water to 1 ounce of salt, or 1,000 grams of water (a liter) to 50 grams of salt. It helps to have a scale when working with large quantities of salt, but Morton's kosher salt has a very close weight-to-volume ratio, so that 2 tablespoons will equal about 1 ounce.

The resulting concentration is the ideal all-purpose brine. It should not be so salty as to feel acrid on the tongue, but should taste like soup that has too much salt in it. It's perfect for pickling (see page 155), for brining a Thanksgiving turkey, a pork chop, or for boiling green vegetables.

One secondary and salutary effect of a brine is that it can actually carry flavors into muscle, so that if you make a brine but also fill it with aromatics, such as onion, carrot, garlic, lemon, and rosemary, a chicken brined for 12 to 24 hours in that brine will pick up the flavors of that brine, the salt carrying them in. Also, the brine changes the cell structure of the meat and can actually result in meat that's juicier than the same cut that hasn't been brined.

Brine—salt liquefied and diluted—is an extraordinary tool.

### Basic Brine

*20 ounces water (2½ cups)*
*1 ounce kosher salt (about 2 tablespoons of Morton's)*

OR FOR LARGER ITEMS

*80 ounces water (10 cups)*
*4 ounces kosher salt (about ½ cup of Morton's)*

Combine the ingredients in a pan over high heat, stirring until the salt is dissolved. Remove from the heat, allow to cool to room temperature, then refrigerate until chilled.

Alternately, you may dissolve the salt in half the water, then weigh the remaining water as ice, and add this to the brine to reduce the cooling time. This method is used in the brined chicken recipe (page 156).


## VARIATIONS

- *Herb and lemon brine for chicken and turkey.* Sauté onion, carrot, and garlic with the salt, add the water, 1 lemon, a bunch of thyme, 1 stem of rosemary, and a tablespoon of cracked peppercorns to the brine, bring to a simmer, then cool and chill completely before using. This will work well with boneless, skinless chicken breasts as well as whole chicken.
- *Garlic-sage brine for pork.* Add a large bunch of thyme, a tablespoon of sugar, 10 cloves of garlic, smashed, and a tablespoon of coarsely cracked pepper to the basic 20-ounce brine. Brine pork chops for 4 to 6 hours, whole loins for 12 to 24 hours.
- *Corning brine for beef brisket and pastrami:* See recipe (page 159).
- *Curing brine for Canadian bacon and smoked ham hocks:* See recipe (page 158).
- *Salted water for all green vegetables.* Use the brine proportion for cooking your vegetables; bring the brine to a rolling boil, then add your vegetables and cook until tender; serve them immediately or shock in ice water, drain, and reheat as necessary.
- *Pickling brine for naturally pickled vegetables:* Make and chill the basic 20-ounce brine. Submerge a variety of vegetables such as cut carrots, cut turnips, and small cucumbers along with some garlic and, if you like heat, some red pepper flakes, in the brine (weight them down so that they are completely submerged), cover them with plastic wrap, and leave at room temperature (75°F or lower) for 1 week (or a few days longer for more sourness). For traditional dill pickles, make a brine with a bunch of dill and a handful of garlic cloves. For a more spicy pickle, add garlic and chillis to the brine. For sauerkraut, submerge shredded cabbage in the plain brine. If you can find very small cucumbers at your farmers' market, make French cornichons by adding garlic, tarragon, and peppercorns to the brine.

### Roasted Chicken with Lemon and Herb Brine
### with Perfect How-to-Cook-Green-Beans Green Beans

Brining chicken is an excellent strategy for infusing the bird with flavor and seasoning, and helping to ensure a juicy breast and crisp skin. Brining is also a preservative, so if you buy a chicken on Monday but can't cook it until later in the week, brining the chicken will keep it fresh. A whole chicken almost always benefits from early salting, whether the salt is in a brine or dry. I include green beans with the recipe, not only because they go well with chicken but in order to discuss how to cook green vegetables. They cook best plunged into brine-strength water that's at a heavy boil. Ideally, the amount of water should be enough relative to the amount of vegetables so that it doesn't lose its boil, but for many home cooks, that's not practical. Nevertheless, it's important to acknowledge that green vegetables are best cooked this way, and should either be served immediately or shocked in an ice bath.

I've tried to make this brine as simple as possible, and the use of ice obviates the need for chilling the brine for hours. Also, it uses a minimum of water to ensure the maximum effect of the aromatics. You're in effect making a quick vegetable stock to brine your chicken in.

FOR THE BRINE

*1 Spanish onion, thinly sliced*
*1 carrot, thinly sliced*
*4 cloves garlic, crushed*
*1½ ounces kosher salt (about 3 tablespoons)*
*1 tablespoon canola oil*
*15 ounces water*
*1 lemon, halved*
*2 bunches of thyme*
*1 branch of rosemary*
*1 bay leaf*

*1 tablespoon black peppercorns, toasted and coarsely cracked*
  *with the bottom of a sauté pan*
*½ ounce sugar (about 1 tablespoon)*
*15 ounces ice*
*One 3- to 4-pound chicken*

FOR THE BEANS

*1 pound green beans*
*Butter as needed*
*½ lemon*

Sauté the onion, carrot, garlic, and salt in the oil in a sauté pan over medium heat until the onion is translucent. Add the remaining brine ingredients (squeezing the lemon halves into the pan, removing any seeds you might see), and bring the liquid to a simmer, stirring until the salt and sugar have dissolved, a minute or so. Remove from the heat and let steep for 10 minutes or longer.

Weigh out 15 ounces of ice and add it to the brine. Stir until the brine is cold and the ice has melted (if it's not completely cool, refrigerate the brine for an hour or until it is).

Rinse your chicken and place it in a 1-gallon plastic bag. Put the bag in a bowl for support. Pour the cold brine and vegetables into the bag with the chicken and seal or tie the bag, trying to remove as much of the air as possible so the chicken is fully in contact with the brine. Refrigerate for 8 to 12 hours, agitating the chicken or turning it over a few times to distribute the brine.

Preheat your oven to 450°F.

Remove the chicken from the brine (discard the brine and vegetables), rinse, and dry it. You can keep the chicken refrigerated, covered, for up to two days before cooking.

Roast uncovered for 1 hour.

Fill a 2-gallon pot with 140 ounces of water (1 gallon plus 1½ cups), add 7 ounces of salt (about a cup), and bring the water to a vigorous boil. Add the green beans. You may cover the pot for 60 seconds or so to help the water return to a boil faster. Boil until the beans are tender (not crunchy), about 4 or 5 minutes. Strain and serve immediately with butter and lemon or shock them in an ice bath, drain, and refrigerate until you're ready to gently reheat them in butter.

Serve them with the chicken, with additional butter or Dijon mustard.

YIELD: SERVES 4

## Canadian Bacon

Canadian bacon is cured, smoked pork loin and is easy to make at home. It doesn't have to be smoked—it will still be delicious if you roast it in an oven, but it does take on smoke flavors well, so if you have a kettle grill, you can smoke-roast it over low indirect heat to make it more interesting and complex. Pork develops its ham flavor from the pink salt, sodium nitrite,* which also keeps the meat a vivid pink even after it's cooked and prevents the growth of harmful bacteria. I'm more comfortable using metric measurements with this quantity of brine, but I've included imperial and volume measurements as well.

*4 liters water (about 1 gallon)*
*200 grams salt (about 7 ounces or a scant cup)*
*200 grams brown sugar (about 7 ounces or 1 cup)*
*40 grams pink salt (1½ ounces, or about 3 tablespoons)*
*4 bay leaves*
*10 cloves garlic*
*1 tablespoon black peppercorns, toasted and coarsely cracked*
*One 2-kilogram (4-pound) pork loin, fat and sinew removed*

Combine all the brine ingredients in a pot large enough to hold the pork loin and bring it just to a boil, stirring to dissolve the salt and sugar. Remove from the heat and allow it to cool to room temperature, then refrigerate until chilled.

---

*Sodium nitrite, often simply referred to as pink salt (it's dyed pink), is a curing salt that's inexpensive and available from www.butcher-packer.com, which sells pink salt under the name DQ Cure.

Place the pork loin in the brine and weight it down with a plate to ensure that it's completely submerged. Refrigerate for 72 hours.

Remove the loin from the brine, rinse it under cold water, and pat dry with a towel. Set it on a rack and refrigerate it for 12 to 24 hours. Discard the brine.

The loin can now be cooked in one of two ways. Canadian bacon is traditionally smoked, but you can roast it in a 200°F oven until it reaches an internal temperature of 150°F. Or it can be smoke-roasted in a kettle grill or home smoker using charcoal and/or wood chips. Build a small, low fire and bank it against one side of the grill. If you're using wood chips for additional smoke, soak them in advance and add them to the coals before cooking the meat. Cook the pork on the opposite side of the grill until it reaches an internal temperature of 150°F.

## Corned Beef

Home-cured beef brisket, or corned beef (so called because of the corn-shaped nuggets of salt originally used to cure the beef), is one of the most remarkable transformations a cook can bring to an ordinary, tough brisket. It's no more difficult than brining a chicken, and the flavor is far superior to store-bought versions. This recipe calls for pink salt, or sodium nitrite.* Its main purpose here is to keep the meat red even after it's cooked; if you omit the pink salt, the beef will turn pot-roast gray-brown, but it will still taste delicious. As previously mentioned, I'm more comfortable using metric measurements with this quantity of brine, but I've included imperial and volume measurements as well.

*2 liters water (½ gallon)*
*25 grams pink salt (1 ounce or 5 teaspoons)*
*50 grams sugar (1¼ ounces, or a scant ¼ cup)*
*10 cloves garlic, flattened with the flat side of a knife*
*100 grams kosher salt (3½ ounces, or just under ½ cup)*

---

*Sodium nitrite, often simply referred to as pink salt (it's dyed pink), is a curing salt that's inexpensive and available from www.butcher-packer.com, which sells pink salt under the name DQ Cure.

*2 teaspoons whole black peppercorns*
*2 teaspoons yellow mustard seeds*
*2 teaspoons coriander seeds*
*2 teaspoons dried red pepper flakes*
*2 teaspoons whole allspice*
*1 teaspoon ground nutmeg*
*1 cinnamon stick, crushed or broken into pieces*
*6 bay leaves, crumbled*
*2 teaspoons whole cloves*
*1 teaspoon ground ginger*
*One 5-pound well-marbled beef brisket*

Combine the water, pink salt, sugar, and garlic in a pot large enough to contain the brisket as well. (Choose a vessel in which the brisket can be submerged but not squeezed in; if you only have a small pot, the brisket can be folded—just be sure to turn it once a day to make sure all surfaces are receiving the brine.) Combine the remaining seasonings in a bowl. Add half these seasonings to the pot and reserve the rest. Bring the water to a simmer, stirring, until the sugar and salts are dissolved. Remove the pot from the heat and allow to cool to room temperature, then refrigerate the brine until it's completely chilled.

Place the brisket in the brine. Weight it down with a plate to ensure the brisket stays completely submerged. Refrigerate it for 4 days.

Remove the brisket from the brine, and rinse it thoroughly under cool running water.

Place the brisket in an appropriately sized pot—not so big that it will float in too much water, but not squeezed in against the sides—and fill the pot with water to cover the brisket. Add the reserved spices along with .25 ounce, or 1½ teaspoons, of salt per quart of water. Bring it to a boil, then reduce the heat, cover, and simmer gently for about 3 hours, or until fork tender (there should always be enough water to cover the brisket; replenish the water if it gets too low). Remove the brisket from the cooking liquid (which can be used to moisten the meat and vegetables, depending on what you're serving), slice, and serve warm.

NOTE: Serve with cabbage seared and then braised in some of the strained cooking liquid, steamed potatoes, and mustard, or slice the brisket for sandwiches, or allow to cool, wrap, and refrigerate until you're ready to serve.

For an excellent variation, you can turn this corned beef into home-cured pastrami by coating the brined but uncooked brisket with a mixture of equal parts ground coriander and ground black pepper, and smoke-roasting it slowly in a kettle grill or home smoker, or grilling it over very low indirect heat, including smoky wood chips, and covering the grill. Steam it till it's tender for hot pastrami.

PART FOUR

# Fat-Based Sauces

Text within the diagram:

MAYONNAISE — OIL — 20 — LIQUID — 1 — YOLK

VINAIGRETTE — OIL — 3 — 1 — VINEGAR

HOLLANDAISE — BUTTER — 5 — LIQUID — 1 — YOLK

# FAT-BASED SAUCES

Fat is flavor.

Fat is texture.

Fat gives dishes succulence, richness.

Fat is the component that makes a dish satisfying, and the fat-based sauces are among the most satisfying preparations in the kitchen and also among the most versatile. A perfect spring asparagus that has been blanched and shocked, so that it's vivid green and tender, is delicious plain. But dipped in a fresh mayonnaise that's seasoned with lemon juice and minced shallot, it becomes delectable. Or a more blunt example: plain lettuce in a bowl is not appetizing, but drizzle it with a shallot vinaigrette made with a delicious olive oil and sherry vinegar and it is.

What makes fat-based sauces so appealing to the home cook, relative to stock-based sauces, is that we always have the base (fat) on hand. Unlike the stock for stock-based sauces, we don't have to make it. Canola oil, olive oil, butter, plus acid and seasoning, and you're good to go. Suddenly that grilled pork chop, that sautéed chicken breast, that steamed cauliflower, those green beans, go from dull to fantastic.

The fat-based sauce is excellent especially with lean preparations—blanched vegetables, lean grilled meat, fish, legumes. But starches and eggs also are elevated by fat-based sauces. (We even like fat-based sauces with fatty dishes—fried fish with tartar sauce, French fries dipped in mayonnaise!)

A word to those who fear fat: *don't.* Fat is good. We need fat to survive. Fat doesn't make us fat (eating more calories than we burn makes us fat). Fat won't make us unhealthy if we eat it in moderation, which happens to be the way it tastes best (you wouldn't want to eat a bowl of vinaigrette or a cup of mayonnaise or a stick of butter). Assuming you have a diet low in processed foods, natural fat used in the proper proportion makes most things better and is good for you.

The following ratios are for the main fat-based sauces: mayonnaise, hollandaise, and the vinaigrette, all of them incredibly versatile, none of them difficult.

# Mayonnaise

**Mayonnaise = 20 parts oil : 1 part liquid (plus yolk)**

This is a revision of the standard ratio in American kitchens and culinary schools. That ratio is easy to remember, and it works, too—1 yolk and 1 cup of oil equals mayonnaise—but the reasoning often taught is that you need that much yolk to emulsify all the oil. In fact, you don't. Think about it: yolk size varies widely, and yet 1 yolk per cup of oil always works, no matter the size of the yolk. So, clearly, the amount of yolk isn't critical.

Harold McGee, in *On Food and Cooking,* notes that there is plenty of emulsifying power in a single yolk: "A single yolk can emulsify a dozen cups of oil or more." Importantly, he goes on, "What is critical is the ratio of oil to water."

The above ratio is updated to account for and underscore the fact that without water (or some form of it, such as lemon juice or vinegar) a handmade mayonnaise is virtually impossible. Mayonnaises can and will break, not if too much oil is added relative to the quantity of yolk, but relative to the amount of water you've included.

An emulsion is formed when the oil is

*Mayonnaise you make at home has a texture and* ▶ *flavor that is simply not possible to mass-produce, which means you cannot buy it. Happily, homemade mayonnaise is easy and inexpensive to make and extraordinarily versatile.*

broken up into countless minuscule orbs that are separated by sheets of water. But what greatly helps the oil and water to remain separate is, among other things, a molecule in the yolk called lecithin, which, McGee explains, is part water soluble and part fat soluble. Lecithin buries itself partly in the yolk (fat) and partly in the water; the water-soluble tail helps to repel other oil droplets and maintain the emulsion. But if there's not enough water, the oil droplets will break through the barrier and join with the other oil droplets and the mixture will quickly turn to an oily soup.

While McGee is the authority on all microscopic culinary matters, and other kitchen scientists confirm his convictions, a kitchen test of small amounts of yolk (as opposed to testing large amounts of oil) did not prove that a small amount of yolk could emulsify an enormous quantity of oil. Working with a cup of oil as the standard measure, I made mayonnaise with ¼ teaspoon of yolk. The results were that it was possible to emulsify about 6 ounces of oil into 1 teaspoon of water and ¼ teaspoon of yolk, before it broke. Using 2 teaspoons of water, I emulsified 7 ounces of oil before it broke. I then used 1 teaspoon of yolk. A mayonnaise using 1 teaspoon of water and that amount of yolk again broke at about 7 ounces. (And I could see ahead of time that it was going to break because the mayonnaise grew very thick and then very shiny.) It may be possible to use smaller quantities of yolk, but given all the things that can go wrong in the process, a healthy teaspoon, rather than a stingy ¼ teaspoon, proved most practical in this experiment.

Of course, there is a color and flavor component to the mayonnaise—using more yolk will give it a deeper color and enhance flavor, important factors in any sauce. It's possible that a cook will have a container of yolks left over from making a meringue or an angel food cake. Were that cook to make a mayonnaise, he or she could simply take a teaspoon or tablespoon of yolk and make the mayonnaise from that. Perhaps you wanted to reduce the quantity of yolk but still have an emulsified sauce—you might measure out a teaspoon or so and discard the rest. But yolks are self-contained and at a little less than an ounce for standard "large" eggs, a convenient size, you would almost always use 1 yolk. If you are making a large quantity—as a chef in a restaurant or for the block party potato salad—you can make all you need with a single yolk, provided you have enough water, about 1 ounce for every 20 ounces of oil (or 10 grams for every 200 grams of oil).

Again, remember that emulsions are more likely to break due to insufficient water than insufficient yolk.

The various ways you might approach a mayonnaise in your kitchen depends on how you cook. You can make a mayonnaise just as you need it or you can make a mayonnaise base and use it as needed, adding seasonings and aromats as the occasion warrants. For instance, if you include minced shallot in your mayo, you'll need to use that mayo that day or it will develop off flavors. But if you make a mayo using only lemon juice and/or water, salt, yolk, and oil, the mixture will be fresh for several days. This way you might make a mayonnaise on Friday afternoon, season half of it with cumin, coriander, minced red onion, and lime juice, and serve it with grilled steaks that night. You might the next day season it with shallot and tarragon for leftover steak sandwiches, and a few days later, season the remainder with *fines herbes* and toss it with sliced new potatoes for a potato salad.

Emulsifying methods vary—a standing mixer, a food processor, some blenders, immersion blenders, and heavy mortar-and-pestles all work. However you wish to do it is fine. I prefer using a whisk because it's quickest—all you need is a bowl and a whisk, no hauling out, then cleaning an appliance—and it gives you more control in terms of the amount, specifically for small amounts (say you want only ¼ cup). If you need a large quantity to feed a big group, you would want to use a standing mixer or something mechanical.

One of the miscellaneous factors in an oil emulsion includes temperature. Room-temperature ingredients encourage emulsification. So does salt. Other ingredients such as mustard help in achieving and maintaining a stable emulsion. Some oils are more emulsion friendly, olive oil over vegetable oil, for instance. But all oils can be emulsified—perhaps the salad calls for a mayo made with walnut oil, or perhaps pistachio oil with lemon juice and zest to serve with a slice of salmon terrine (page 145).

Knowing the ratio and base techniques frees you in the kitchen.

Troubleshooting. Mayonnaises can be the Difficult Child, beloved in spite of their misbehavior, breaking into gloop just as you are about to finish. Sauces can sense when you're afraid of them, so don't be. Mayonnaises can and will break on you and sometimes you simply have to let them. But ultimately you can and must take that broken mayonnaise and reemulsify it. Eventually it will learn. To reemulsify a broken mayonnaise, get a new bowl, add a teaspoon of water (and, if you wish, a little more egg yolk), and begin adding the broken mayo to the water while whisking continuously until you have a properly disciplined sauce.

### Basic Mayonnaise: An Exceptionally Versatile Sauce

Mayonnaise is one of the great pleasures for the cook because of the transformation brought to bear on ordinary vegetable oil. It's a metamorphosis, and you, the cook, are a sorcerer. You begin with a clear, viscous, flavorless liquid and, with a little acid and salt, a whisk and a yolk, create a heavenly sauce of creamy consistency and satisfying flavor. It's remarkable. You'd never want to dip that tender green bean in vegetable oil—but transform that oil into a lemony mayonnaise, and suddenly you do.

The following is a basic mayonnaise, seasoned with lemon juice and salt. But even this is more ornate than is necessary. If you truly wanted a blank canvas on which to paint, you could make a mayonnaise with 1 teaspoon of yolk, a tablespoon of water, and 10 ounces of oil. So remember that the following mayonnaise even before you add additional spices or aromatics is variable. Perhaps you would like to use a white wine vinegar as the acidic/liquid component, or red wine vinegar or lime juice or Meyer lemon juice or verjuice. A mayonnaise base will keep for a week if well wrapped (the fat can absorb refrigerator odors).

This is a perfect all-purpose mayonnaise, excellent on its own and also easy to elevate toward virtually any dish that benefits from fat and flavor.

> 1 large egg yolk, preferably organic or farm-raised
> ½ teaspoon salt
> 1 teaspoon water
> 2 teaspoons fresh lemon juice, or to taste
> 7 to 10 ounces canola or vegetable oil (about 1 cup)

Combine the yolk, salt, water, and lemon juice in a large bowl (the bigger, the better, even for a small quantity of oil). Twist a dish towel into a ring around the base of the bowl to keep the bowl from moving as you whisk in the oil. Measure out your oil in a cup from which you can pour it in a steady stream, such as a 1-cup Pyrex measuring cup (a cup of oil weighs 7 ounces). Begin whisking the yolk, then drizzle in a few drops of oil while whisking, followed by a few more drops of oil to establish the emulsion. Whisking continuously, add the remaining oil in a thin stream. The mixture should be thick enough to cling to your whisk. If you can pour it, the mixture has broken. If this happens, pour the broken mayonnaise back into the oil cup, wipe out your bowl, and add a teaspoon of water to the bowl (and a little extra yolk if you have it). Pour the broken mayonnaise drop by drop into the teaspoon of water while whisking rapidly to establish the emulsion, then continue to add the broken mayonnaise in a thin stream.

YIELD: 1 CUP

Once you know the ratio and technique, it's a matter of minutes to create a custom-made sauce for whatever meat or vegetable you may be serving. Variations are infinite. Use your common sense in terms of flavor pairing. Perhaps one of the best aromats in a mayonnaise is finely minced shallot. I hate to do without it. I like to make a very shalloty, very lemony mayonnaise, allowing the shallot to macerate in the lemon for a few minutes, in order to soften its flavor, before whisking in the oil. The same method using garlic and olive oil will give you a traditional aioli (classically, oil is emulsified into the liquid using a heavy mortar and pestle)—use a cup of good fruity olive oil and a teaspoon of very finely minced garlic; allow the garlic to macerate for a few minutes in the lemon juice.

Please note: when using raw garlic in a mayonnaise, it's important to remove the germ, the living, often green, shoot within the clove, which can give the garlic an off flavor. Slice the clove in half lengthwise and, using a paring knife, remove the germ. If you're preparing a lot of garlic, unpeeled cloves can be halved and soaked in warm water, which facilitates both peeling and removing the germ. This is generally good practice, but not required if you're cooking the garlic immediately.

You might serve some salmon with that lemon-shallot mayonnaise, or instead you might ask yourself what flavors go well or are common with salmon. Dill is often paired with salmon, as are chives—so you might make a dill-chive mayonnaise. This would go perfectly with potatoes as well. Citrus flavors go well with salmon—you could make a citrus mayonnaise with zest from lemon, lime, grapefruit, and orange along with some of their juices.

I wouldn't season lamb with dill; for a lamb sandwich you might instead season a mayonnaise with mint or cilantro. Aromatics and seasoning can be added to the liquid before the oil or after, though it's best to add green herbs after the oil is added so that the acid doesn't discolor them. If you want to make a curried chicken salad with leftover roast chicken, add fresh (or freshly made) curry powder, with some finely minced garlic and finely grated ginger. Or you might go in another direction with *fines herbes*. Or in another direction with ginger, minced scallions, a drop of fish sauce, and a little sesame oil. Mustard is a ready and excellent seasoning for mayonnaise. Experiment with various oils, walnut or pistachio. There's no end to the possibilities.

### Lemon-Shallot Mayonnaise

This is my favorite variation, an aggressive use of lemon and a pinch of cayenne. It goes with any manner of chicken or fish or vegetables, crudité, or à la grecque, and there's nothing better with a steamed and chilled artichoke.

> *1 tablespoon lemon juice*
> *1 tablespoon finely minced shallot*
> *½ teaspoon salt*
> *1 large egg yolk*
> *⅛ to ¼ teaspoon cayenne*
> *7 ounces canola oil (1 cup)*

Combine the lemon juice, shallot, and salt in a large bowl and let sit for a few minutes. Twist a dish towel into a ring around the base of the bowl to keep the bowl from moving as you whisk in the oil. Add the yolk and cayenne and whisk to combine. Measure out your oil in a cup from which you can pour it in a steady stream, such as a 1-cup Pyrex measuring cup. Begin whisking the yolk, then drizzle in a few drops of oil while whisking, followed by a few more drops of oil to establish the emulsion. Whisking continuously, add the remaining oil in a thin stream. Taste and adjust for seasoning. Evaluate for consistency—if it's too thick, a little water or lemon juice can be added to thin it if you wish.

YIELD: I CUP

## Chilli-Lime Mayonnaise

This is a great mayonnaise to serve with grilled pork and grilled beef, or for sandwiches made from grilled meat. The quantities below are suggestions. You might add any number of different ground chilli peppers depending on what's available to you. Just make sure they're fresh, not old and insipid. If you buy whole dried peppers, toast them in an oven to fully dehydrate them, remove stems and seeds, and grind in a coffee mill or spice grinder. Taste your hot spices before you add them to gauge how spicy they are.

> 2 teaspoons cumin seeds, toasted and finely ground
> 1 teaspoon coriander seeds, toasted and finely ground
> ⅛ teaspoon cayenne or ground chipotle powder
> 1 clove garlic, germ removed, finely minced or crushed or
>   crushed to a paste
> 2 teaspoons fresh lime juice, or to taste
> ½ cup Basic Mayonnaise (page 169)
> 1 tablespoon chopped cilantro
> 1 teaspoon minced jalapeño (optional)
> Salt and freshly ground black pepper

Combine all the ingredients except the salt and pepper and season to taste with salt and pepper. It's best to make this at least an hour before you serve it to allow the spices to bloom.

YIELD: ½ CUP

## *Mayonnaise with* Fines Herbes

This is a versatile and delicious sauce for chicken, cold or warm, or for a chicken salad. It's delicious on potatoes as well. Boil some new potatoes, allow them to cool until you can handle them, slice them thinly, and top with this *fines herbes* sauce. Perfect for warm summer evenings. Chervil can be difficult to find; it's fine to double the tarragon if chervil is unavailable.

> *1 teaspoon chopped tarragon*
> *1 teaspoon chopped chervil*
> *1 teaspoon chopped parsley*
> *1 teaspoon chopped chives*
> *1 teaspoon minced shallot*
> *½ cup Basic Mayonnaise (page 169)*
> *Salt and lemon juice to taste*

Combine the herbs, shallot, and mayonnaise. Taste and adjust the seasoning with salt and lemon juice as necessary.

YIELD: ½ CUP

## *Curried Mayonnaise*

This variation can be used with any meat that is traditionally curried—chicken, lamb, shrimp—as well as for vegetables. Using bold flavors is important when serving food cold, to compensate for the aromatic boost hot foods have in their favor. Be sure to use very fresh curry powder (not stuff that's been sitting in your spice rack for years). For additional flavor, heat it in a dry pan, transfer it to another container to allow it to cool, then add it to the mayonnaise.

> *2 teaspoons curry powder*
> *¼ teaspoon cayenne (optional)*
> *1 clove garlic, germ removed, crushed or finely minced*

*1 teaspoon finely grated ginger*
*½ cup Basic Mayonnaise (page 169)*
*Salt and lemon juice to taste*

Combine all the ingredients except the salt and lemon juice and stir to combine. Season to taste with the salt and lemon juice. It's best to let this rest refrigerated for a half hour to allow the seasoning to bloom, then taste and reseason if necessary.

YIELD: ½ CUP

## Instant Mayonnaise

For a small quantity of fresh mayonnaise, ½ cup or so, there is a wonderfully simple, incredibly fast method using an immersion blender, a process first described to me by Bob del Grosso, a chef I correspond with frequently. It's almost unfair that I wait until the end of the chapter to reveal a method faster than a whisk, but I think it's important to whisk as well. This method results in a very thick mayonnaise, but it's also more easy to break than one made with a whisk. That notwithstanding, an immersion blender and a cup just big enough to fit the blade end of it is all you need for perfect mayonnaise in a flash. So there's no excuse to reach for the Hellmann's if you want a fresh aioli for crudités or a chilli mayo for a grilled pork sandwich. Or, no, not even that. Next time you make a BLT, take 3 minutes extra to make this mayonnaise. It will be the best BLT you've ever made.

*1 large egg yolk*
*1 teaspoon water*
*1 teaspoon lemon juice*
*¼ teaspoon salt*
*½ cup canola oil (or more as you need it, adjusting the lemon juice accordingly)*

Combine the yolk, water, lemon juice, and salt in a 2-cup Pyrex measuring glass. Buzz it once with an immersion blender to mix. Add a few drops of oil, holding the blender to the bottom of the cup and blending until an emulsion forms, 2 to 3 seconds. With the blade running, pour the remaining oil slowly into the cup, beginning to lift the immersion blender up and down to incorporate all the oil. Once you start blending, the process should take 15 to 20 seconds.

YIELD: ½ CUP

# Vinaigrette

## Vinaigrette = 3 parts oil : 1 part vinegar

A vinaigrette is such a useful concept, it should be considered a mother sauce, given its own category in the classical sauce repertoire, and regarded as a tool almost in the same way as stock. The vinaigrette may be the most commonly used of all of the sauces—both in the home and in professional kitchens. Its mixture of fat, aromatic flavors, spices, and acid has unusual power and influence over a dish. Fat conveys not only richness and luxuriousness but also carries the flavors of the aromatics, seasonings, and spices; acid, one of the fundamental flavor components of any dish, brings contrast to fatty dishes (such as grilled meats) and complexity to lean or neutrally flavored ingredients, such as lettuces, vegetables, and fish.

And like other mother sauces, the vinaigrette is infinitely variable, not only in your choice of seasonings and aromats but in your choice of fat and your choice of acid, which doesn't necessarily have to be vinegar. All decisions are influential. A neutral oil is probably the most common, but if olive oil is used, the vinaigrette moves in a different direction; if warm

*The vinaigrette is so important, so useful to the* ▶
*cook, so versatile in what it enhances, from fish to meat to vegetables, and so mutable in terms of its flavors, it deserves to be considered a mother sauce. It's second only to salt in terms of its use as a seasoning device. Here a basic vinaigrette with shallots is spooned over cooked leeks.*

bacon fat replaces the oil, the differences are even more distinct. The acid is usually a vinegar, obviously, and in this case there are many choices—red or white wine, or sherry or balsamic, or a flavored vinegar. But verjuice, the juice of unripe wine grapes, might be the acid, or citrus juice, lime or grapefruit—and it would still fall under the rubric of a vinaigrette. Aromats range from sweet shallot and soft-stemmed herbs (basil, chives, parsley, mint, cilantro, dill), which should be added just before serving, to hard-stemmed herbs (sage, rosemary, oregano, thyme), which should be allowed to infuse the vinaigrette for an hour or more, to chilli powders and curries (best toasted before being added).

How they are mixed also determines the final effect of the sauce. At its simplest, a vinaigrette is oil and vinegar added separately to a salad (add the oil first to coat the leaves, then "season" them with the vinegar). They can be whisked or blended so that the oil and vinegar temporarily combine, but the sauce remains loose. Or the oil can be emulsified into the acid for a thick and creamily textured sauce. And like the mayonnaise, the vinaigrette can be made in quantity as a base and used as needed throughout the week, adding to it any variety of aromat and seasoning you wish.

The ratio of 3 parts oil or fat to 1 part acid is standard but can and should be varied according to your tastes. For a vinaigrette using red wine vinegar, 3 to 1 is perfect, but for a sharp citrus juice, such as lime juice, you may want to use 4 parts oil. For a sharper, leaner vinaigrette, or if using a powerfully flavored fat such as duck fat or bacon fat, you may want to reduce the ratio of the fat. Another way to reduce the quantity of oil is to add a lot of other ingredients—blend in a fresh tomato for a tomato vinaigrette. Or you might substitute a vegetable stock for some of the oil to reduce the calories in the vinaigrette.

Vinaigrettes are perfect for salad greens and vegetables, of course, but they also pair perfectly with all manner of poultry, fish, and meat. For example, a grapefruit vinaigrette for poached salmon, a chilli vinaigrette for grilled steak. A classic South American sauce for beef, the chimichurri (page 182) is nothing more than a heavily herbed vinaigrette. You might sauté some shallot in the fat rendered from the chicken you've just sautéed, deglaze with some vinegar or lemon juice, add some chopped tomato, and spoon this over the chicken for what is an *à la minute* warm vinaigrette. Warm vinaigrettes are excellent with fish as well. The vinaigrette is a friend to all, and it's a smart cook who consciously acknowledges the power of the vinaigrette and uses it as a lever in his or her cooking.

## Classic Red Wine Vinaigrette

This is the workhorse vinaigrette, a great all-purpose dressing for salads and vegetables. White wine or lemon juice can be substituted, and garlic (raw or roasted) and black pepper can be used as aromats. Aromats such as minced shallot (or roasted shallot) or freshly chopped parsley can be added at the last minute to vinaigrettes using wine vinegars. And often you may want to introduce some form of sugar or honey to balance the acidity. In this recipe, mustard is added both for flavor and because mustard helps to maintain an emulsion.

The standard method is this: all the ingredients except for the oil are combined (it's important that the salt be allowed to dissolve in the vinegar so that it's distributed evenly), then the oil is slowly whisked or blended in to create a homogeneous sauce, as with a mayonnaise. If the oil is added all at once, it will quickly separate. The harder it is whisked or blended, the thicker it will become. You can emulsify your vinaigrette by whisking in the oil or by pouring it in a thin stream into a running blender. If you use a blender, though, it may become too thick to blend, in which case you'll need to remove it from the blender into a bowl and to finish emulsifying the oil with a whisk. Needless to say, the better tasting your vinegar, the better your sauce—with vinegar, you tend to get what you pay for.

*2 ounces red wine vinegar (about ¼ cup)*
*1 tablespoon Dijon mustard*
*¼ teaspoon salt, or to taste*
*6 ounces canola oil (about ¾ cup)*

Combine the vinegar, mustard, and salt in a bowl or a blender. While whisking continuously or blending, add the oil in a slow stream until all the oil is incorporated. This vinaigrette will keep refrigerated for a week.

YIELD: 1 CUP

## VARIATIONS ON THIS ARE ENDLESS

- Replace the red wine vinegar with white wine vinegar or sherry vinegar—the better the vinegar, the better the vinaigrette.
- Add a sweet note with a tablespoon of honey, brown sugar, or balsamic vinegar.
- Add freshly chopped herbs, 2 tablespoons of minced parsley or chives or a combination along with a tablespoon of minced shallot before using.
- Add 1 roasted shallot to the vinegar and puree in a blender as you add the oil. (To roast, wrap an unpeeled shallot in foil with a few drops of olive oil and a pinch of salt and cook in a 400°F oven until tender, about 30 minutes.)
- Add other vegetables to your standard vinaigrette: add ⅓ cup of diced roasted red beets to the vinegar and puree as you add the oil for a sweet beet flavor and a vivid color.
- Add ½ cup of cherry tomatoes to the vinegar and puree as you add the oil for a more complex acidity and sweetness.
- For a vinaigrette with Asian flavors, for a cucumber salad, julienned daikon, or any kind of slaw, add 1 tablespoon peeled, finely grated ginger to the oil and allow it to infuse for an hour or more. Then replace the red wine vinegar with rice wine vinegar, and the Dijon mustard with 2 teaspoons ground mustard, and season with a teaspoon of sesame oil.

### Citrus Vinaigrette

Citrus vinaigrettes are refreshing, can use less oil depending on the acidity of the fruit used, and work well with soft greens, as well as vegetables cooked and chilled such as leeks.

*¼ cup fresh grapefruit juice*
*2 tablespoons lime juice*
*1 tablespoon fresh orange juice*
*¼ cup red or Vidalia onion, small diced*

*½ teaspoon lime zest*
*½ teaspoon orange zest*
*¼ teaspoon salt*
*4 ounces canola oil (about ½ cup)*

Combine all the ingredients except the oil in a bowl and slowly whisk in the oil.

YIELD: ABOUT 1 CUP

## *Nut Vinaigrette (Walnut)*

Nuts add, yes, a nutty dimension to vinaigrettes. You can make a nut vinaigrette simply by using a flavorful nut oil as your fat, or you can add roasted and chopped nuts to the vinaigrette as you blend it, either pureeing them in the blender or leaving them chunky. The following vinaigrette would go perfectly with an endive, watercress, and apple salad, or with any other crisp, sharp lettuces. Other nuts and oils you might use for nut vinaigrettes include pistachio (and pistachio oil) and pecan (and pecan oil). Use good oils—often they can be rancid. La Tourangelle is a company that makes very good nut oils (http://www .latourangelle.com).

*¼ cup sherry vinegar*
*¼ teaspoon salt*
*3 ounces canola oil*
*3 ounces walnut oil*
*¼ cup walnuts, toasted and coarsely chopped*

Combine the vinegar and salt in a bowl and whisk in the oils, then the nuts. Alternately, the vinegar, salt, and nuts can be combined in a blender and the oils can be added in a thin stream while the blender is running.

YIELD: ABOUT 1 CUP

## Vinaigrettes for Meat and Fish

Here are a few vinaigrettes that are designed not for dressing salads or vegetables, but rather meat. Though they do go well with salad, their big flavors enhance and flavor meat and serve as an excellent strategy for saucing your dish with something other than a reduced stock and butter.

### *Chimichurri Sauce*

The chimichurri is a South American preparation, a heavily herbed vinaigrette typically paired with beef. It should have the consistency of a loose pesto. I think oregano should always be a part of the chimichurri, but you can vary the herbs, of course. Add cilantro, add mint. Want more heat? Add another jalapeño or some minced chipotle.

> ¼ cup red wine vinegar
> ½ teaspoon salt
> 6 ounces olive oil (about ¾ cup)
> 3 tablespoons chopped oregano
> 3 tablespoons chopped parsley
> 1 tablespoon red onion, small diced
> 1 teaspoon minced garlic
> 1 jalapeño pepper, stemmed, seeded, and small diced
> 2 teaspoons hot smoked paprika

Combine the vinegar and salt to dissolve the salt. Add the remaining ingredients. Allow the sauce to sit for an hour so that the aromatics infuse the oil.

YIELD: A LITTLE MORE THAN A CUP

## Lime-Peanut Vinaigrette

The lime-peanut vinaigrette gets a good portion of its fat from the peanut butter, thus the change in the basic ratio. This vinaigrette works especially well with chicken. America pretty much has a lock on pressing chicken on a salad, and this vinaigrette would be excellent that way, or on chicken alone, but lime and peanut flavors also go well with beef and pork. So consider replacing the boneless chicken breast with grilled flank steak and this dressing.

> ¼ cup lime juice
> ½ teaspoon salt
> 1 tablespoon minced shallot
> ¼ cup natural peanut butter
> ¼ teaspoon cayenne
> 4 ounces peanut oil or vegetable oil (about ½ cup)

Combine the lime juice, salt, and shallot in a blender. Blend for a second or two to dissolve the salt and distribute the shallot. Add the remaining ingredients and blend until they're combined.

YIELD: I CUP

## Warm Tomato Vinaigrette

This is a basic vinaigrette, only instead of being cold, it's mixed together in a medium-hot pan, which intensifies the flavor of the tomato and the sweetness of the shallot. This is a great sauce for whitefish, halibut or cod or tilapia (and would do wonders for the ubiquitous boneless chicken breast). But it also works well with boiled new potatoes, salt cod, or a combination of boiled new potatoes, or other root vegetables, and salt cod or smoked trout.

> ½ cup tomatoes, seeded, peeled, and diced
> ½ teaspoon salt, or to taste

*¼ cup sliced shallot*
*1 teaspoon minced garlic*
*1 tablespoon canola oil*
*1 tablespoon Dijon mustard*
*1 ounce sherry vinegar (2 tablespoons)*
*2½ ounces olive oil (about 5 tablespoons)*

Toss the tomatoes with the salt to begin drawing out their moisture and flavor. Sauté the shallot and garlic in the canola oil over medium-high heat until translucent. Add the tomatoes and any liquid that's leached out to the pan and cook, stirring, for a minute or so, to heat the tomatoes and reduce some of the liquid. Add the mustard and vinegar and stir to combine. Whisk in the olive oil until incorporated, then remove the pan from the heat. Taste for seasoning, and add salt or vinegar as needed. Spoon over fish, chicken, or vegetables.

# Hollandaise

**Hollandaise = 5 parts butter : 1 part yolk : 1 part liquid**

The emulsified butter sauces—hollandaise and béarnaise are the most common today, and rightfully so—remain among the glories of the sauce world, emblems of a cook's craftsmanship and the bear-hug love for that great culinary element, butter. An emulsified butter sauce should be thick and luxurious, deeply flavored with aromatics from shallot to fresh herbs, and distinctly acidic with lemon juice or vinegar. It should be bright and vibrant in color and should feel light on the palate.

These sauces get much of their richness from lots of egg yolk whipped over heat. The traditional ratio, not by weight, is excellent and works beautifully: hollandaise = 1 pound butter : 6 yolks. This ratio seems to have originated with Escoffier. Some cookbooks call for considerably less butter per yolk, as little as 3 and some even closer to 2 to 1, but then you're creeping into sabayon territory; what's more, I believe it's a cook's moral obligation to add more butter given the chance. Like the traditional mayonnaise ratio, the hollandaise ratio hasn't before taken into account the water. To review this wisdom, discussed in

*Emulsified butter sauce is like a mayonnaise, only ▶ it's hot and uses butter rather than oil. It's one of the most luxurious and rich sauces a cook can create. Here a traditional béarnaise sauce, a sauce flavored with fresh tarragon, graces a grilled steak.*

the mayonnaise chapter, McGee writes that there is more than enough lecithin in a single yolk to emulsify many ounces of fat. So additional yolk in a hollandaise, or any of the emulsified butter sauce siblings, is for texture, flavor, and richness. We also know that the chief danger to the emulsion is not having enough water (which includes lemon juice and vinegars). Water content is an even more precarious situation in these sauces because, unlike a mayonnaise, the sauce is cooked (and thus continuously giving up its water as it vaporizes during the cooking). So the yolk quantity is not as critical to the ratio as the water. As a rule, I like to have about a tablespoon of water per 10 ounces of fat to ensure a stable emulsion. When making a hollandaise, I usually keep some water on hand to drizzle in if needed.

The standard ratio translates to a weight ratio of approximately 5 parts butter to 1 part yolk and 1 part water (more water than you need in a mayonnaise, again, because you need to cook the eggs for several minutes, during which water is cooking off ). The yolk of large eggs weighs about .6 ounce. Five yolks, or 3 ounces of yolk and water, would be used for 15 ounces of butter (or in metric measurements, 50 grams yolk and water for every 250 grams of butter). Again, the ratio is helpful for reducing the quantity of finished sauce. If you don't want to make a lot of sauce, you can just use 1 yolk (.6 ounce) and 3 ounces of butter (85 grams).

After that, it's all about flavor: seasoning with herbs, aromatics, spices, and acid.

The principle underlying emulsified butter sauce is the same as that of mayonnaise. Fat, in this case butterfat (traditionally pure butterfat, or clarified butter) rather than oil, is whipped into egg yolk to create a thick, stable emulsion. They differ from mayonnaise in several important ways. First, they're warm sauces, meant to be eaten with hot food. The egg yolk is cooked, which contributes voluminous body and flavor to the sauce. The quantity of egg yolk is typically higher in an emulsified butter sauce than in a mayonnaise, which makes it richer in color, texture, and flavor. And the acidic component often includes a reduction: vinegar is reduced with aromats, then strained and included in the final sauce as part of the water. But as with a mayonnaise, the quantity of egg yolk in traditional recipes far exceeds what you need to form a stable emulsion. A little bit of yolk can emulsify many cups of oil; the critical factor is having enough water in the sauce to maintain the emulsion.

I've written both the traditional hollandaise, the one you learn in books and in culinary school—6 yolks per pound of butter, an excellent easy-to-remember ratio—as well as less-conventional sauces. If you want to create a very pure butter flavor, you can reduce the quantity of yolk, but the yolk is still an important ingredient in terms of the finished flavor; if you love the impact of the fluffy, frothy egg, you can add less butter.

Traditionally, clarified butter is used, but whole butter can be used as well. Clarified butter results in a very refined and delicate flavor. Whole butter contains water and other solids, so will help to maintain the emulsion. On the other hand, your ingredients are warm, and as you cook the eggs, you lose water, so take care to ensure enough water—whether it's water, the reduction, or acid—remains in the mixture to maintain the emulsion.

The method is standard: Make your reduction with the appropriate aromats and vinegar, strain it into your cooking vessel (a double boiler ensures gentle heat, but you can use direct low heat if you wish), add salt (salting early is important to ensure it dissolves), add the yolks, and cook the mixture, whisking continuously, until the eggs are fluffy and cooked (150°F to 160°F). Reduce or remove from the heat and whip in the butter as you would oil for a mayonnaise, then add fresh aromats and additional seasoning such as lemon juice as necessary. Some people choose to strain the emulsified sauce before adding the final aromats, which will remove any bits of cooked egg, should there be any.

Of course, these sauces are famed for breaking and throw fear even into the most intrepid of home cooks. The addition of heat makes them more precarious in terms of stability than the mayonnaise. The heat is causing a few things to happen that you don't need to worry about in a mayonnaise. First, it's cooking the eggs and so the egg molecules are transforming—you can overcook your egg and wind up with bits or even chunks of egg in your sauce. And it's resulting in some water loss. Water is a critical component in an emulsion because it's what separates the minuscule orbs of oil from one another, a condition that results in a thick, creamy sauce. So depending on how hot your sauce is, the rate at which it's losing water varies. It's rarely a bad idea to add a few more drops of water as you whisk to make sure you have enough.

Do not be afraid of its breaking. Sauces can sense fear and will use it to their mischievous advantage. I have broken many sauces and am still a happy, productive member of society and an advocate of the emulsified butter sauces. If you make them, you can and will break them. When this happens, all you have to do is fix it. First, admit defeat, accept that this will tack on 5 or 10 minutes of cooking (infinitely worth it), and request a best-of-three rematch. I have never lost a best-of-three. Ever.

Simply get another yolk and a couple of teaspoons of water, warm them a little, and start adding your broken sauce the way you added the butter. You'll have your sauce back in no time. And it's even more satisfying to have been brazenly challenged by your sauce and to have been undaunted.

These sauces cannot be served piping hot, but should be served warm. The best way to make these a little bit ahead of time is to hold them in a thermos (this works with other sauces as well, of course). Or keep them in a warm place, but not over direct heat, until ready to serve, pressing some plastic wrap onto the surface to keep a film from forming. For reasons of food safety, don't hold them for more than an hour or so like this.

Leftover sauce must be refrigerated and the butter will harden. The sauce is a great medium in which to scramble eggs, or it can be melted and reemulsified as you would with a broken sauce, or even into a tablespoon of hot water.

Variations on the emulsified butter sauce, while many, are not quite so vast as varying mayonnaise because the butter-and-egg combination is such a rich and dominant part of the sauce. So when improvising on the hollandaise, stick to pairings that work well with butter. The classics are classics for a reason. They work. Hollandaise is the plain mayonnaise version of the emulsified butter sauce, its dominant seasoning being lemon. Can't beat it. The béarnaise, perhaps my all-time-favorite sauce, is seasoned with tarragon. Abundant fresh tarragon is best (though I grew up in a family that made it with dried tarragon and tarragon vinegar in the reduction and no fresh tarragon, which was not widely available in the 1970s Cleveland grocery store). Choron sauce is a béarnaise enhanced with tomato puree and typically paired with fish. Maltaise is a hollandaise flavored with orange. *Sauce valois* is a béarnaise with highly reduced beef or veal stock added. For a mousseline sauce, fold about half as much whipped cream in. The following recipes are for the classics, with a couple of ideas for variations. A béarnaise, and a *sauce paloise,* which is flavored with mint. The main reason I like mint is because it grows like a weed all summer long and so it's abundant. It's somewhat problematic in that it doesn't go with as many things as the workhorse herbs—thyme, parsley, and tarragon. But it does go nicely with some dishes. Lamb is classically paired with mint, so a *sauce paloise* is a perfect match for grilled lamb chops. Béarnaise is traditionally paired with beef, filet mignon, but it's fantastic on boiled potatoes or sautéed chicken.

Citrus juices and zest can lighten a béarnaise, reduced meat stocks can add depth, and whipped cream can be folded into it, in which case it is classically called a mousseline sauce.

### Classic Hollandaise Sauce

A by-the-book, how-they-teach-it-in-culinary-school hollandaise—hard to beat this. Perfect and very elegant for asparagus, salmon, and, of course, poached eggs.

> *2 tablespoons cider vinegar*
> *5 peppercorns, cracked with the bottom of a sauté pan*
> *4 teaspoons water*
> *½ teaspoon salt*
> *2 ounces yolks (or 3 large egg yolks)*
> *10 ounces warm clarified butter (2½ sticks)*
> *2 teaspoons lemon juice, or to taste*
> *Cayenne to taste (optional)*

Combine the vinegar and peppercorns in a small pan and reduce over medium-high heat by about half. Strain into a metal or Pyrex bowl or double-boiler insert. Add the water and salt and stir to dissolve the salt. Add the yolks. Place the bowl or insert in an appropriately sized pan or double boiler partly filled with hot water (the water shouldn't touch the bowl or insert) and bring the water to a simmer, whisking the yolk mixture continuously. When the yolks have doubled or tripled in volume, remove the double boiler from the burner and begin whisking in the warm clarified butter in a thin stream until it's all incorporated and the sauce is thick and creamy. If the sauce becomes very thick and shiny, almost as if the water is being squeezed to the surface, or if you sense the sauce is about to break, add a teaspoon of cold water or lemon juice. When the butter is incorporated, taste and add more lemon juice as needed. Add cayenne if using.

This sauce can be kept warm for an hour in a thermos, or in the pan—press plastic wrap onto its surface to keep the heat in and prevent a skin from forming. Don't leave it covered on any heat, or it will break.

For a citrus butter sauce, add 2 tablespoons of grapefruit juice, 1 tablespoon of lime juice, and a teaspoon each of grapefruit, lime, and orange zest.

For a hollandaise mousseline, whip 2 ounces of cream to soft peaks. Fold this into the hollandaise.

YIELD: IO TO I2 OUNCES

## Sauce Béarnaise

This is my choice for best sauce ever created and it is a personal favorite of my mom. In her determination to get as much butter as possible into her sauce, she raised sauce making to the level of a sporting event. I grew up before fresh herbs were widely available and so was used to dried tarragon, but fresh tarragon can't be beat for the most vibrant flavor. I don't clarify a lot of butter and so I simply use whole melted butter.

> 2 tablespoons white wine vinegar
> 2 tablespoons white wine
> 5 tablespoons chopped tarragon
> 5 peppercorns, cracked with the bottom of a sauté pan
> 1 tablespoon minced shallot
> 4 teaspoons water
> 2 teaspoons lemon juice, or to taste
> ½ teaspoon salt
> 2 ounces yolks (3 large egg yolks)
> 10 ounces butter (2½ sticks), melted

Combine the vinegar, wine, 2 tablespoons of the tarragon, the peppercorns, and shallot in a small pan and reduce over medium-high heat by about half. Strain into a saucepan or Pyrex bowl or double-boiler insert, pressing the solids to squeeze out the liquid. Add the water, lemon juice, and salt and stir to dissolve the salt. Add the yolks. Place the bowl or insert in an appropriately sized pan or double boiler partly filled with hot water (the water shouldn't touch the bowl or insert) and bring the water to a simmer, whisking the yolk mixture continuously. (If you're using a saucepan, cook the yolks over medium heat, being very careful not to scramble them.) When the yolks have doubled or tripled in volume, turn off the heat. Add a few drops of butter, followed by a few more drops of butter, whisking until it's completely incorporated and the emulsion has been established. Add the remaining butter in a thin stream, whisking continuously until it's all incorporated and the sauce is thick and creamy. If the sauce becomes very thick and shiny, almost as if the water is being squeezed to the surface, or if you sense the sauce is about to break, add a teaspoon of cold water or lemon juice. If the sauce is thick enough, it's never a bad idea to add a little water to ensure you have enough—though remember that whole melted butter has water in it, so when using melted butter, you'll need to add less water than if you're using clarified butter. When the butter is incorporated, taste and add more lemon juice as needed. Fold in the remaining 3 tablespoons tarragon just before serving.

This sauce can be kept warm for an hour in a thermos, or press plastic wrap onto its surface to keep the heat in and prevent a skin from forming. Don't leave it covered on any heat, or it will break. If you find you need to reheat it, do so in the same way you cooked it, over gentle heat, whisking as it reheats.

For *sauce choron,* finish the béarnaise sauce with 4 ounces of tomato sauce or a tomato puree. Serve with lean grilled or sautéed fish.

For *sauce paloise,* replace the tarragon with mint, with an additional tablespoon of chopped mint added at the end. Serve with lamb or fish.

For a béarnaise mousseline, fold in half as much cream, whipped to soft peaks. Serve with a hearty whitefish such as monkfish, cod, halibut, or sablefish.

YIELD: 10 TO 12 OUNCES

## *Chipotle-Cilantro Butter Sauce*

Classic hollandaise and béarnaise sauces require several steps—clarifying butter, making the reduction, and completing the sauce, but there's no reason the process can't be simplified. Here's a way of doing just that. Gather all your *mise en place,* and a sauce will come together as soon as the steaks and corn on the cob are off the grill. All the ingredients except for the butter are combined in a saucepan, the eggs are cooked over direct heat, and the melted butter is whisked in (melt it in a measuring cup or a cup with a spout). The milk solids and water will sink to the bottom of the butter container—these can be whisked in as well, if you wish, or discarded. The point here is to make an emulsified butter sauce *à la minute.* This is an excellent sauce for any grilled meat, especially beef.

> *3 tablespoons lime juice*
> *1 tablespoon water*
> *1 tablespoon minced shallot*
> *2 to 3 chipotle peppers in adobo sauce, seeded and finely*
> *    chopped (about a tablespoon)*
> *½ teaspoon salt*
> *2 ounces yolks (3 large egg yolks)*
> *10 ounces butter (2½ sticks), melted*
> *2 to 3 tablespoons chopped cilantro*

In a small saucepan, combine all the ingredients except the butter and cilantro. Whisk them over medium heat until the yolks double in volume and become fluffy (if you sense they're cooking too fast or that you're losing too much liquid, add water until the mixture is smooth). Remove from the heat, and whisk in the butter in a thin stream. Add the cilantro and stir until combined.

YIELD: IO TO I2 OUNCES

## Red Wine and Rosemary Sauce

Some good red wine and hearty herbs can be all you need to take the emulsified butter sauce in a different direction. I've halved the amount here to serve four, but it can be doubled for more, and I suggest cooking this in a saucepan to make it quicker.

*½ cup good, big red wine (Zinfandel or Pinot Noir)*
*1 tablespoon shallot, minced*
*1 tablespoon rosemary, finely minced*
*¼ teaspoon salt*
*1 ounce yolks (2 large egg yolks)*
*5 ounces butter, melted*
*Lemon juice (optional)*

Combine the wine, shallot, rosemary, and salt in a small saucepan (one with a rounded bottom is best for cooking the yolks). Reduce the wine over medium-high heat until it is almost dry. Add a tablespoon of water to the pan, along with the yolks, and whisk over medium-low heat until the yolks have doubled in volume and become frothy (this should take several minutes; be careful not to cook the yolks too fast). When the yolks are cooked, add the butter a few drops at a time, then in a thin stream, whisking continuously. Taste for seasoning. Add a squeeze of lemon, more salt, or more minced rosemary to taste.

YIELD: 6 OUNCES, 2 TO 4 PORTIONS

# PART FIVE

# The Custard Continuum

# CUSTARD

The egg and dairy concoction we call custard—whether in a savory quiche, a stand-alone crème caramel, or a pourable vanilla sauce—has an incomparable capacity to satisfy, perhaps more than any single preparation. It is rich, flavorful, nutritious, and, properly prepared, a wonder on the palate. It can be rustic or refined, served in four-star dining rooms, or as a weekday dessert at home. It can be savory or sweet, served pure and plain, or loaded with ingredients. It takes on myriad forms across the globe—from chowan mushi in Japan, to Spanish flan, to flans made with coconut milk throughout Southeast Asia, to French quiche, to English bread pudding. It can be the very embodiment of luxury and refinement and yet it is made with the most common and economical ingredients in the kitchen. The custard represents the ultimate transformation of the egg.

The key to a custard's excellence is texture. You should be able to see its satiny smoothness the moment you dip into it, and it should hit the palate like cream that is not cream, cream that is more substantial than cream, cream in its very best form (even though there may be no cream in it). And the key to this texture is proper cooking. Custards are often cooked in a water bath, or bain-marie, to ensure that the temperature of the vessel they're cooking in doesn't get hotter than 212°F and the egg cooks gently. If a custard gets too hot, the egg proteins bunch up and the custard curdles and sets with a porous spongy texture and eggy feel. The only way to ensure that custards don't overcook is to pay attention, keep an eye on them. Make custards often and you will know how long they generally take. You'll begin to recognize the right jiggle that signals you to pull them out of the oven; it shouldn't be liquidy when you jiggle the dish, the custard continuing to move after the dish stops moving. But nor should it be so cooked that there is no jiggle—that's overcooked. It should be gently set at the outside and seem to have just crossed over the line between liquid and solid, but the center should still have a little jiggle to it. Remember that it will continue to cook after it's removed from the oven, so you actually need to remove it when it's not quite done.

Custards can be cooked uncovered, but they will develop a skin that is slightly tougher and darker than the rest of the custard. For a crème caramel, which will be upended onto a plate, or a crème brûlée, which will get a crust of browned sugar on top, a skin does not necessarily need to be prevented. But if you are serving the custard as is and don't want a skin, then you should cover the custard, or the water bath, so that it bakes in a moist environment (parchment topped by aluminum foil to keep it in place is good for this; some brands of plastic wrap can be used, or any material or lid that will not collect moisture that will drip down into the custard).

As with most fundamental preparations, the custard has a continuum based on what ingredients go into it and how much of each, relative to the others. They can be grouped into three distinct categories, and it's useful to think of custard in these terms: free-standing, in a vessel, and as a sauce.

Custards that are freestanding need a little more structure, which is provided by egg white, so dishes such as quiche, crème caramel, and cheesecake usually include whole eggs. Custards that are served in a dish require less structure, and so may use only egg yolk—crème brûlée and pot de crème, for example—and are cooked in their serving vessel in a water bath. Custard sauces, based on crème anglaise, use only yolks and are cooked on the stovetop. This sauce can be served immediately as a warm vanilla sauce, thickened with starch so that it has body (pastry cream), or chilled in an ice bath to use cold or to freeze into ice cream.

As with doughs and batters, the egg/milk combination we call custard is the trunk from which different branches extend—the savory custard (quiche, for example), the sweet custard (crème caramel), and vanilla sauce. From vanilla sauce extends more branches—pastry cream, ice cream, and crème brûlée. Mastering the custard is one of the pleasures of learning to cook. It's a skill that expands your range in the kitchen exponentially.

# Custard, Free-Standing

## Free-standing custard = 2 parts liquid : 1 part egg

The standard ratio is bedrock, 2 to 1; 16 ounces milk blended with 8 ounces (4 large) eggs will result in 24 ounces of an excellent custard. Large eggs are about 2 ounces each, which makes custards easy to manage without a recipe: a cup of milk and 2 eggs, or ½ cup of milk and 1 egg.

But 1 large egg will set three-quarters of a cup of milk into a perfect custard. So, as with all ratios, and recipes, it can vary. If you intend to turn the custard out and it needs to hold its shape, stick with the basic ratio. Extra yolks are often added for texture and richness. The quantity of sugar and the quantity of fat also affect the final outcome. If you're using a lot of sugar, you may need to add a little more protein for structure. If you're using only heavy cream, you may need less.

Custards can be flavored with anything, from vegetables to sweets; it all depends on where and how you want to serve them. You might make a leek custard as a garnish for a beet soup, a bone marrow custard to accompany a grilled steak. You might make a tarragon custard—garnished with diced orange, it would be an elegant starting

*Custards can be divided into three categories—▶ custards that are pourable, custards that are so delicate, they must be served in a dish or container, and custards that have enough body, they can stand on their own, as this one does, a traditional crème caramel.*

course—or a rosemary custard or mint custard to serve with leg of lamb. In classical French cuisine, a custard can be diced and used as a garnish in consommé, in which case it's called a royale. Escoffier lists numerous flavorings for royales, including carrots, celery, asparagus, leek, chestnut, chicken, and others, which, again, illustrates the versatility of the custard. This is classical cuisine, but you might make a chilled English pea soup and garnish it with a carrot royale, diced or ring cut, for a peas-and-carrots soup that wouldn't be out of place on a contemporary American fine dining menu.

Quiches are custards baked in a crust that are usually loaded with interior garnish (bacon and onion for a Lorraine, spinach for a Florentine, but anything that goes with egg could be used—sausage, diced ham, plenty of cheese, roasted peppers). They make a great meal at any time of the day.

Custards shine brightest on the sweet side of the meal—crème brûlée and caramel, pot de crème, crème anglaise, and vanilla ice cream. They're very easy, but, again, proper cooking is the critical element of finesse in the stand-alone custard.

## *Classic Crème Caramel*

Crème caramel is a freestanding custard that's unmolded onto a plate and the caramel, which has liquefied, coats the top and spills onto the plate. It's one of my favorite dishes for its simplicity, practicality, deliciousness, and elegance. And it's got its own simple ratio: 2 : 1 : ½— milk, egg, sugar, flavored with a pinch of salt, and a teaspoon of vanilla or a vanilla bean. Crème caramel can be prepared in a large baking dish and served family style, but it's most elegant when prepared in individual 4-ounce ramekins. This recipe will make 6 portions; the custard can be increased or decreased in 2-ounce/1 egg increments.

FOR THE CARAMEL

*½ cup sugar*
*2 tablespoons water*

FOR THE CUSTARD

*2 cups milk*
*8 ounces eggs (4 large eggs)*
*½ cup sugar*
*1 teaspoon vanilla extract*
*¼ teaspoon salt*

Combine the ingredients for the caramel in a small pan over medium heat and cook until the sugar has melted and becomes an appealing brown. If it foams up, take it off the heat and let it calm down so that you can evaluate the color and doneness. Pour it into your ramekins. It should coat the bottom to about ⅛ inch. Allow it to cool completely into a hard candy.

Preheat your oven to 325°F. Place the ramekins in a large ovenproof sauté pan or a roasting pan and fill the pan so that the water comes three-quarters of the way up the sides of the ramekins. Remove the ramekins and place the pan of water in the oven.

Combine the ingredients for the custard and blend until the mixture is uniform (this can be done with a whisk, a hand blender, or a standing blender). Fill the ramekins evenly, about 3 ounces each. Place the ramekins in the water bath in the oven. Bake for 30 to 40 minutes, until the custards are almost set. Remove them to a rack to cool, then refrigerate until thoroughly chilled, several hours at least.

To serve, loosen the edges where the custard adheres to the ramekin with the tip of a knife and turn them out onto plates.

YIELD: 6 SERVINGS

## Quiche Lorraine

The quiche has been misunderstood in America since it crossed the Atlantic from France and tried to fit itself into a store-bought pie shell. A proper quiche shell must be deep enough to allow you to cook the custard properly, which is why it is traditionally made in a 2- by 9-inch ring mold. Ring molds are inexpensive and can be found in many kitchenware stores, but you might also use a 2-inch cake pan, provided you line the

*The quiche is an example of a preparation in which a freestanding custard carries abundant internal garnish, such as bacon, onion, and cheese in this classic quiche Lorraine. The standard pie dough is blind baked in a 2-inch-deep ring mold. The depth is critical in achieving a custard with a luxurious texture.*

bottom with parchment paper. If you cook a custard in a pie shell, even if you cook the custard perfectly and don't overcook it, which is easy to do when it's so thin, the custard is too shallow to offer its fundamental pleasure, which is a luxurious texture.

A quiche can be garnished inside with anything that goes well with eggs. Traditional garnishes include spinach and mushrooms, but you might just as easily replace those with roasted poblano peppers and Mexican chorizo. Cheese is usually a component, and for the former, you'd use a Comté or similar cheese, but for the latter, you might use Jack cheese.

I learned how to make quiche while working on the *Bouchon* cookbook with Thomas Keller, Jeffrey Cerciello, and Susie Heller. I have made many quiches since then and done all I can to elevate the quiche to its proper status in the American home kitchen. It's an extraordinary dish. It can be made a day or more ahead of serving it. It can be served hot or cold and can be served for any meal of the day, breakfast, lunch, dinner, or late-night supper.

This recipe is for a classical quiche Lorraine, which designates a bacon and onion garnish, my favorite quiche.

*2 large Spanish onions, thinly sliced*
*Canola oil as needed*
*3-2-1 Pie Dough (page 24)*
*1 pound slab bacon, cut into ¼-inch lardons\**

---

\*Lardons are batons of bacon but can be as thick as ½ inch square. Smaller lardons are best here, but a pound of thick-cut bacon sliced into strips is also acceptable.

*2 cups milk*
*1 cup cream*
*10 ounces egg (6 large eggs)*
*2 teaspoons kosher salt*
*½ teaspoon freshly ground black pepper*
*Nutmeg to taste (about 5 gratings)*
*½ cup grated Comté or Emmental cheese*

Sauté the onions over medium heat in a film of canola oil. You might cover them for the first 15 minutes to get them steaming and releasing their moisture, then uncover, reduce the heat to medium-low, and continue cooking them until they are cooked down but not overly brown, 45 minutes to an hour. Set them aside when they're finished.

Preheat your oven to 350°F. Roll out the dough to a thickness of about ¼ inch. Place a 2- by 9-inch ring mold or a 9-inch round cake pan on a baking sheet (line the baking sheet with parchment if you're using a ring mold; if you're using a cake pan, also line its bottom with parchment). Lightly oil the inside of your ring mold or pan. Lay the dough into the mold—there should be plenty of dough overhanging the edges to help it maintain its shape. Reserve a small piece of dough to fill any cracks that might open in the dough as it bakes. Blind bake the dough until the crust is golden brown (line the dough with parchment or foil and fill it with dried beans or pie weights so that the crust bakes flat, but don't dock the dough if you normally do this; after a half hour, remove the weights and parchment of foil, gently patch with the reserved dough any cracks that may have formed, and continue baking until the bottom of the crust is golden and cooked, about 15 more minutes). Remove it from the oven and patch any cracks that may have opened; this is especially important if you're using a ring mold, or the batter may leak out. The shell should be anywhere between cold and warm when you add the batter, not piping hot from the oven.

Reduce the oven temperature to 325°F.

Sauté the bacon gently until it's cooked as you like it (crisp on the outside, tender on the inside, is best!). Drain the bacon and combine it with the onions.

In a 6- or 8-cup liquid measure, combine the milk, cream, eggs, salt, pepper, and nutmeg and, using a hand blender, blend until frothy. This can be done in a standing blender as well (though depending on the size of your blender, you may need to divide the quantities in half). Or you could even mix the batter in a large bowl using a whisk (beat the eggs first, then add the rest of the ingredients). The idea will be to add the ingredients in two layers, using the froth to help keep the ingredients suspended.

Layer half of the onion-bacon mixture into the shell. Pour half the frothy custard over the mixture. Sprinkle with half the cheese. Layer with the remaining onion-bacon mixture. Refroth the batter and pour the rest into the shell. Sprinkle the remaining cheese over the top. You may want to put the tray with the quiche shell into the oven and pour the remaining batter into it there so that you can get every bit of batter into the shell. You can even let it overflow to make sure it's up to the very top. Bake in the 325°F oven for about 1½ hours, or until the center is just set (it may take as long as 2 hours, but don't overcook it—there should still be some jiggle in the center).

Allow the quiche to cool, then refrigerate it until it's completely chilled, 8 hours or up to 3 days.

Using a sharp knife, cut the top of the crust off along the rim. Slide the knife along the edge of the ring mold or cake pan to remove the quiche.

Slice and serve cold, or, to serve hot, slice and reheat for 10 minutes in a 375°F oven on lightly oiled parchment or foil.

YIELD: SERVES 8 TO 12

## What You Can Do Now
## That You Have the Custard Ratio

As the quiche demonstrates so well, custards are wonderful when made with savory ingredients and it's really here, on the savory side, that the custard ratio shows its extraordinary versatility.

Anything that can be made into a soup can just as easily be transformed into a custard, for instance. Mushrooms, leeks, sweet bell peppers, beets, carrots, all make wonderful custards. Green vegetables such as peas and asparagus can be blanched and shocked and used as the flavoring medium of a custard. Herbs also make excellent custards simply by infusing a straight custard with flavor. Or you might try flavoring a custard with something more exotic, such as bone marrow. Or a different kind of fat, such as a flavorful olive oil. Such custards can be unmolded and served standing or served in the ramekin. Or they can be baked in a baking dish, then cut in the desired shapes, and used as garnish. If you're serving them warm, reheat them in a 325°F oven for 5 to 10 minutes.

When improvising on the savory custard, remember to stick to 2 parts liquid to 1 part egg to ensure you have the right consistency. You can use half-and-half or add some cream for a more voluptuous texture. You can cook them in a ramekin and serve them in the ramekin. Or you can use flexible silicone molds or foil baking cups, which makes unmolding them easier.

A custard can be used to fill a tart shell when you want to feature the garnish so that rather than being a distinct feature itself as it is with the quiche, it serves only to hold the ingredients together, as with the savory leek and walnut tart (page 27) and the sweet blueberry "clafouti" tart (page 29). Or you might go further by binding that leek and walnut tart with a caramelized onion custard. To make a wild mushroom tart, you might incorporate mushrooms into the custard.

Another variation on this idea of a custard binding ingredients is to use a sweet custard with bread—leftover bread is just a custard away from a delicious bread pudding.

Here are some suggestions:

- *Sweet bell pepper custard.* Cut 1 red or yellow bell pepper in a large dice (discarding seeds and white ribs), about 8 ounces. Simmer in 1 cup of half-and-half with ½ teaspoon of salt until tender. Puree in a blender and strain through a fine-mesh strainer. You should have about 1½ cups (incidentally, replace the half-and-half with cream, and this can be served at this stage, after blending and straining, as a red pepper soup). Return this to the blender and add 1 egg for every ½ cup of liquid, about 3 eggs in this case, with the blender running. Taste for seasoning and add more salt if necessary; add a pinch of cayenne if you wish. Pour into your baking vessel and cook in a water bath as with crème caramel (page 200) just until set. This will be enough for 4 to 6 portions.

- For mushroom, carrot, beet, turnip, celery root, leek, caramelized onion, or custard from any other nongreen vegetable that strikes your fancy, follow the method for a sweet bell pepper custard, but replace the bell pepper with 8 ounces of the vegetable of your choice.
- *Asparagus custard.* Cook ½ pound of asparagus in brine-strength water (page 153), then shock in ice water, cut into ½-inch pieces, and reserve the tips for garnish. Combine the asparagus stalks with 1 cup of half-and-half with 1 teaspoon of salt and blend in a blender until completely smooth. Strain the mixture through a fine-mesh strainer. Return it to the blender and add an egg for every ½ cup of liquid. Bake in a water bath as with the crème caramel (page 200). Unmold and serve topped with the reserved tips and a squeeze of lemon or an ounce of hollandaise (page 189).
- For variations on the green vegetable custard, replace the asparagus with fresh English peas, snap peas (with pods), or spinach.
- For a bone marrow custard, soak 10 ounces of bone marrow (removed from the bone) in water for 24 hours. Bring a cup of half-and-half, a teaspoon of salt, ½ teaspoon of cracked peppercorns, and ½ teaspoon of coriander seeds, toasted and crushed beneath a sauté pan, to a simmer and remove from the heat. Poach the marrow in simmering water for 3 to 4 minutes. Combine the half-and-half, marrow, and 2 eggs in a blender and blend until the mixture is uniform. Strain it through a fine-mesh strainer, pour into ramekins, and bake in a water bath as for crème caramel (page 200). Garnish with fleur de sel.
- *Herb custards.* For herb custards, include hard-stemmed herbs such as rosemary and sage. Add the herb to the liquid, then heat the liquid and allow the herb to infuse it—a tablespoon of chopped rosemary, a very strong herb, or ¼ cup of sage for each cup of liquid. When using soft-stemmed herbs for custards— mint, basil, tarragon or *fines herbes,* chives—add ½ cup of the herb to the blender and pour the hot cream over them, blend thoroughly, adding 2 eggs per cup of liquid as you do so. After blending, strain and pour into your ramekins or baking dish, cover, and cook in a water bath.
- A sweet custard, the crème caramel ingredients (see page 201), will

hold fruit such as blueberries, or a combination of blueberries and raspberries, in a tart shell; and a savory custard, which doesn't use sugar or vanilla, will hold savory ingredients, such as caramelized onions and anchovies, leek and walnut, or traditional quiche ingredients. The point of the tart, though, is not the custard, as it is with the quiche, but the garnish, so tarts should have abundant garnish that's bound with the custard. It's important to blind bake your tart shell, reserving some tart dough in case any cracks develop; patch the cracks to prevent the custard from leaking out. Set your tart pan on a baking sheet, fill it with your ingredients, pour in the custard (you'll need about 2 cups for a 9-inch tart pan), and bake at 325°F until set.

- A great garnish can be leftover bread. Make a bread pudding by adding a teaspoon of cinnamon and ½ teaspoon of nutmeg to the crème caramel custard (see page 201). Remove the crust from day-old bread, cut the bread into large dice, lay the bread in a baking dish, and pour the custard over it. Allow the bread to soak up the custard for 15 minutes or so, pressing down on the bread to encourage absorption. Bake in a water bath until the custard is just set, 30 to 45 minutes. Serve warm with some warm crème anglaise (page 211). Another great sauce option is to use the unfrozen Maker's Mark ice cream recipe as the sauce (page 213).

# Crème Anglaise— the Amazing All-Purpose Dessert Sauce

**Crème Anglaise = 4 parts milk/cream : 1 part yolk : 1 part sugar**

Crème anglaise, also known simply as anglaise, or vanilla sauce, or custard sauce, is among the simplest, quickest dessert preparations in the kitchen and is so basic in its dairy-and-yolk structure that it can become any number of finished dishes, depending on how it's handled. The most common and unadulterated results of cooking vanilla-infused milk and cream with egg yolks (crème anglaise) are crème brûlée and vanilla ice cream. Adding fat or starch or protein will create popular variations: cornstarch results in pastry cream; adding butter to that gives you buttercream; adding whipped cream and gelatin gives you Bavarian cream; chocolate and whipped cream gives you chocolate mousse. And, of course, vanilla sauce takes all kinds of flavorings, from brown butter to sweet spices to distilled spirits, for infi-

*Crème anglaise—egg yolks, milk and cream, sugar ▶ and vanilla—is heated on the stovetop until the eggs are cooked and the sauce has thickened. It should be strained immediately into a bowl set in ice to remove any large particles or cooked egg for a satiny texture and to halt its cooking.*

*The four variations on crème anglaise: crème pâtissière, thickened with starch; ice cream, thickened by freezing; crème brûlée, thickened by baking; and crème anglaise, or custard sauce, thickened by cooking on the stovetop.*

nite variations. But here I want to focus solely on these few wonderful products.

The crème anglaise ratio above is simplified and measured by weight; a yolk is .6 ounce, or about ½ ounce, so this amounts to 4 yolks per 8 ounces dairy; it's a richer, slightly sweeter version than a more common dairy-to-yolk ratio, which is 3 yolks per cup of liquid. If you are making a quart of custard, 12 yolks results in an excellent sauce. So an alternate *volume* ratio that works well is 1 cup of milk/cream : 3 yolks : 3 tablespoons of sugar.

Whichever ratio you use, do what you should always do in the kitchen: pay attention. Remember the results. Think about how small variations in the ratio will give you the nuances you want. Fewer yolks will result in a looser consistency. Using all cream will counteract that somewhat. Use less sugar if you want your sauce less sweet. Use your common sense.

## Crème Anglaise

Vanilla sauce, the workhorse dessert sauce, is incredibly simple to make, incomparably delicious, and easily manipulated into infinite flavors and forms. It can be served warm with a soufflé or apple tart or cold over fresh berries or frozen into ice cream. Crème anglaise is simply this: a combination of milk and cream, sweetened with sugar, flavored with vanilla, enriched with and thickened by egg yolk. At its most pure and clean, the vanilla comes solely from a bean (1 bean will flavor up to 24 ounces of dairy). But given good dairy and eggs, even a teaspoon of imitation vanilla extract in whole milk is delicious straight off the spoon.* Depending on how rich you want it, more cream can be used. Though many think that whole milk is plenty rich.

*8 ounces milk (1 cup)*
*8 ounces cream (1 cup)*
*1 vanilla bean, split down its length*
*4 ounces sugar (about ½ cup)*
*4 ounces yolks (7 large egg yolks)*

---

*Cook's Illustrated*'s *The New Best Recipe* describes a taste test of imitation and natural vanilla extract and the tasters unanimously favored the imitation.

Combine the milk, cream, and vanilla bean in a saucepan and bring to a simmer. Remove from the heat and let the bean steep for 15 minutes. With a paring knife, scrape the seeds from the pod into the milk-cream mixture. Discard the pod or store it in sugar for vanilla-scented sugar.

Combine the sugar and yolks and stir vigorously with a whisk for 30 seconds or so (this will help the sugar to begin dissolving and will also help the egg to cook more evenly).

Fill a large bowl with a 50–50 mixture of ice and water, and place a second bowl in the ice bath. Set a fine-mesh strainer in the bowl.

Over medium heat, bring the milk-cream mixture just to a simmer, then pour it slowly into the yolks while whisking continuously. Pour the mixture back into the pan and continue stirring over medium heat until the mixture is slightly thick, or *nappé*—it should be completely pourable, but if you dip a spoon in it, it should be thick enough on the spoon to draw a line through it—2 to 4 minutes, depending on how hot your burner is.

Pour the sauce through the strainer into the bowl set in the ice bath. Stir the sauce with a rubber spatula until it is cold. Cover and refrigerate until ready to use.

YIELD: ABOUT 2 CUPS

An intriguing variation on crème anglaise, one that is considerably less common than ice cream and crème brûlée, is Bavarian cream, which is anglaise stabilized with gelatin and lightened with whipped cream. Bavarian creams are used in molded desserts and can be used for layering cakes. To make Bavarian cream, add ¼ ounce of gelatin (about a teaspoon, bloomed in a tablespoon of water and heated in a hot oven or microwave until the gelatin is melted) to 1 cup of fresh crème anglaise. Cool the sauce in an ice bath until it's about room temperature, then fold in a cup of heavy cream that's been whipped to soft peaks. Bavarian creams can be flavored with chocolate, lemon or other citrus juices, distilled spirits and liqueurs, ground praline, and fruit purees. It can be chilled in molds and served with more cream or fruit puree or it can, while still warm, before it sets up, be spread on alternating layers of sponge cake (page 63), and chilled. The cake can then be finished with whipped cream or buttercream (see page 216).

## Vanilla Ice Cream with Maker's Mark

Once you have the above custard sauce, ice cream is a matter of popping it into your machine. I like to flavor ice cream any number of ways, here with bourbon. But you might just as easily flavor it with brown butter and toasted almonds, a caramel sauce, or cherries. If you were thinking ahead, you might infuse the milk-cream mixture with sliced ginger and orange zest before making the sauce. Again, understand the principle and the ratio, and you're limited only by your taste and imagination.

This particular ratio reduces the quantity of yolks to that of the alternate ratio, but it's still more yolks than most ice cream bases. I love the texture and richness that results. Also the alcohol contributes to the softness and texture of this ice cream.

*1½ cups milk*
*1½ cups cream*
*1 vanilla bean, split down its length*
*¾ cup sugar*
*6 ounces yolks (9 large egg yolks)*
*2 to 4 tablespoons Maker's Mark bourbon, or to taste*

Combine the milk, cream, and vanilla bean in a saucepan and bring to a simmer. Remove from the heat and let the bean steep for 15 minutes. With a paring knife, scrape the seeds from the pod into the milk-cream mixture. Discard the pod.

Combine the sugar and yolks and stir vigorously with a whisk for 30 seconds or so (this will help the sugar to begin dissolving and will also help the egg to cook more evenly).

Fill a large bowl with a 50–50 mixture of ice and water, and place a second bowl into the ice bath. Set a fine-mesh strainer in the bowl.

Over medium heat, bring the milk-cream mixture just to a simmer, then pour it slowly into the yolks while whisking continuously. Pour the mixture back into the pan and continue stirring over medium heat until the mixture is slightly thick, or *nappé*—it should be pourable, but if you dip a spoon in it, it should be thick enough on the spoon to draw a line through it—2 to 4 minutes, depending on how hot your burner is.

Pour the sauce through the strainer into the bowl set in the ice bath. Stir the sauce with a rubber spatula until it is cold. Add the bourbon to taste. Cover and refrigerate until the sauce is thoroughly chilled, preferably overnight. The colder it is before going into the machine, the better.

Freeze according to your machine's instructions.

YIELD: ABOUT 3 ½ CUPS ICE CREAM

## *Crème Brûlée*

This is a classic version, very rich and very smooth, flavored only by the pure vanilla bean. This ratio results in what I think is the optimum texture.

*1 cup milk*
*1 cup cream*
*1 vanilla bean, split down its length*
*4 ounces sugar (about ½ cup), plus sugar for coating*
*4 ounces yolks (8 large egg yolks)*

Preheat your oven to 325°F. Place 4-ounce ramekins in a large ovenproof sauté pan or a roasting pan and fill the pan so that the water comes three-quarters of the way up the sides of the ramekins. Remove the ramekins and place the pan of water in the oven.

Combine the milk, cream, and vanilla bean in a saucepan and bring to a simmer. Remove from the heat and let the bean steep for 15 minutes. With a paring knife, scrape the seeds from the pod into the milk-cream mixture. Discard the pod.

Combine the 4 ounces (½ cup) sugar and the yolks and stir vigorously with a whisk for 30 seconds or so (this will help the sugar to begin dissolving and will also help the egg to cook more evenly). Pour the milk-cream mixture into the yolks slowly while whisking continuously.

Pour the custard into your ramekins. Bake in a covered water bath: you can either cover each individual ramekin or cover the water bath itself; I've found covering first with parchment paper followed by foil works best. Cook the custards until just set, about 30 minutes. Allow to cool. If you intend to serve the custards the following day, refrigerate them until chilled, then cover with plastic wrap; remove from the refrigerator several hours before serving to allow to come to room temperature. (Depending on the kitchen environment, a cold custard can develop condensation on the top, making the brûléeing uneven.)

Top each custard with enough sugar to coat the entire surface, and pour off the excess, about ¼ cup. With a propane torch, heat the sugar until it melts, bubbles, and caramelizes—when it's cool, the browned sugar should create a delicate crust.

YIELD: SERVES 4

## Crème Pâtissière

This is a rich and clean delicious pastry cream, the likes of which you rarely find in America anymore—too often it's a processed gelatinous imitation. This is the real deal, and you could eat it like the best vanilla pudding if it weren't so rich! It's best as an accompaniment, such as in the profiteroles (page 48).

*8 ounces plus 3 ounces milk*
*8 ounces cream*
*1 vanilla bean, split down its length*
*4 ounces sugar (about ½ cup)*
*4 ounces yolks (8 large egg yolks)*
*6 tablespoons cornstarch*
*2 ounces butter (½ stick)*

Combine the 8 ounces of milk, the cream, and the vanilla bean in a saucepan and bring to a simmer. Remove from the heat and let the bean steep for 15 minutes. With a paring knife, scrape the seeds from the pod into the milk-cream mixture. Discard the pod.

Combine the sugar and yolks and stir vigorously with a whisk for 30 seconds or so (this will help the sugar to begin dissolving and will also help the egg to cook more evenly).

Fill a large bowl with a 50–50 mixture of ice and water.

Combine the cornstarch with the 3 ounces of milk and stir to disperse the cornstarch.

Over medium heat, bring the milk-cream mixture just to a simmer, then pour it slowly into the yolks while whisking continuously. Pour the mixture back into the pan and add the cornstarch-milk mixture, then continue stirring over medium heat until the mixture just hits a boil and becomes very thick. Sink the base of the pan into the ice bath and continue stirring until the mixture has cooled slightly but is still warm enough to melt the butter. Add the butter and stir until it's completely incorporated. Transfer to a bowl, cover with plastic wrap, pressing the wrap against the surface, and refrigerate until ready to use.

A variation on crème pâtissière is a miraculous all-purpose buttercream used for icing cakes and cookies. While there are many different types of buttercreams, for a simple version, simply whip an equal amount of room-temperature butter into the pastry cream until they are combined.

YIELD: ABOUT 2½ CUPS

## Profiteroles with Hot Chocolate Sauce

This is a classic French bistro dessert, essentially cream puffs with a warm chocolate sauce, and is a great one for entertaining because all but the hot chocolate should be done ahead of time. You can plate the dish while the cream heats and the chocolate melts. The cream is simply sauce anglaise that has been frozen (ice cream) or that has been thickened with a slurry (pastry cream). I prefer the pastry cream—one, because it's less common and, two, because it's easier to plate. (Alternately, the profiteroles can be filled with the pastry cream and dipped in the chocolate sauce for éclairs.)

As with so many bistro dishes, this shows how the deepest pleasures come from the simplest ingredients.

*1 recipe* pâte à choux, *sweet, baked into 24 profiteroles*
   *(page 48)*
*1 recipe pastry cream (page 215) or ice cream (page 213)*
*1 recipe chocolate sauce (page 221)*

Slice the profiteroles widthwise. Place 3 bottoms on each plate, spoon the pastry cream or the ice cream onto each one, and cover with the tops. Pour the warm chocolate sauce over the profiteroles.

YIELD: SERVES 8

# Chocolate Sauce and Caramel Sauce

**Chocolate Sauce = 1 part chocolate : 1 part cream**

**Caramel Sauce = 1 part sugar : 1 part cream**

Chocolate sauce (chocolate and cream) and caramel sauce (sugar and cream) are so fundamental that they are almost always finessed in one direction or another in terms of flavor and texture. But they have easy baselines, general proportions to use as a springboard, and once you know them, you have an infinite array of variations, depending on the type of confection you want to make.

Chocolate sauce, also known as ganache, is made with equal parts chocolate and cream and is so easy, it almost doesn't count as a technique. Simply pour hot cream over an equal weight of chocolate. Let the chocolate melt for a few minutes, then whisk the cream until all the chocolate is incorporated. The mixture looks at first like a badly broken sauce, but the chocolate easily blends with the cream into a gorgeous, glossy, voluptuous sauce.

*Sugar cooked until it melts and browns takes on ▶ wonderful and complex flavors. This straight caramel, used for a crème caramel, will harden, but adding cream and butter to it will create a rich, opaque, pourable caramel sauce.*

When this sauce cools, it will be stiff and so makes an excellent coating for cakes and fruits or it can be rolled into chocolate truffles.

Other sugars or fats can be added or withheld to change the consistency and feel—corn syrup or butter, for instance, or more cream can be added for a sauce that pours cold or less cream for a stiffer ganache. Milk or even water can be used. The flavor, too, can be taken in any number of directions by infusing the cream as you heat it, vanilla or ginger or fruit zest, or by adding flavors such as a spirit, liqueur, or fruit juice.

The variations become a matter of taste and experimentation. Indeed, there is only one hard-and-fast rule for chocolate sauce: you must use good chocolate, a bittersweet or semisweet chocolate that tastes delicious on its own. After that you can hardly go wrong. In fact, some homemade chocolate sauce poured over vanilla ice cream made from a basic crème anglaise (page 211) gives a pleasure that is ethereal in its simplicity and deliciousness.

Caramel sauce can likewise be taken in any number of directions and is also as flexible as ganache. Because of this, and the fact that sugar behaves differently depending on how hot you get it before adding the cream, one might argue that there isn't a single caramel ratio—but a 1 : 1 ratio is a useful baseline. Sugar is melted in a dry pan (or with some water to dissolve it first), cooked until it's a deep amber color, and then cream is added. For clear caramel sauces, a clear liquid can be added. Often the sauce includes butter or is finished with butter. But, again, the basic enriched caramel sauce is endlessly variable. Use half the cream for a thicker, sweeter sauce. Use milk and butter, flavored milk or cream with vanilla, or with rum, or add a few drops of lemon juice or cider vinegar.

One of my favorite variations on the caramel sauce is butterscotch sauce. In this variation brown sugar is used and butter is cooked in the caramel, which adds a distinctive nutty, complex flavor to the sauce from the cooked butter solids. Vanilla is an additional flavor, and some demand salt (caramel and salt is a felicitous pairing). I like to add a few drops of apple cider vinegar to sharpen the sweetness. As far as I can discover, this is not a traditional facet of butterscotch sauce, but when I first read in one source that vinegar gives butterscotch its distinctive flavor, I was so intrigued that I continued to use it even though most butterscotch recipes I've found don't call for any acid whatsoever. I should say, what few recipes I've been able to find. Butterscotch recipes are scarce. Why is this? Do we no longer make it? Do we not think it's special? My guess is that we've gotten so used to store-bought sauce and imitation-flavored chips that we've forgotten how special it can be.

Both the caramel sauce and the chocolate ganache are extraordinarily easy—it's difficult to understand how we became so reliant on bottled sauces.

## *Basic Ganache*

This is perhaps the simplest dessert sauce imaginable, so much so that it's a wonder that bottled chocolate sauce even exists. The texture is exquisite and the flavor is rich. This can be used as a sauce (it will need to be warmed—microwaving is fine—before serving if you've chilled it in the refrigerator) for ice cream or profiteroles (page 48). It can be rolled, cold, and dusted with cocoa powder for truffles. It can be used to coat cakes and brownies for a fudgelike icing. Choose a good brand of chocolate such as Scharffen Berger or Callebaut.

> *8 ounces cream*
> *8 ounces delicious bittersweet or semisweet chocolate, coarsely*
> *chopped*

Bring the cream just to a simmer, pour it over the chocolate, wait 5 minutes for the chocolate to soften, then whisk the cream and chocolate until they're completely combined. Serve immediately or chill until you're ready to serve.

YIELD: ABOUT 2 CUPS

*Ganache, or chocolate sauce, is not only one of the* ▶
*most delicious sauces there is, but also the easiest to*
*make—simply pour hot cream over an equal weight*
*of chocolate, let it sit a moment, then stir to combine.*

## Variations on Basic Ganache

### Rum-Cardamom Chocolate Sauce

*8 to 10 cardamom pods, split or cut in half*
*One 1-inch piece of ginger, peeled and thinly sliced*
*8 ounces cream*
*1 ounce light or dark rum*
*8 ounces delicious bittersweet or semisweet chocolate,*
    *coarsely chopped*

Combine the cardamom, ginger, and cream in a small pan. Bring the cream to a simmer, remove it from the heat, and cover. Allow the pods and ginger to steep for 30 minutes. Gently reheat the cream, add the rum, and strain over the chopped chocolate.

YIELD: A LITTLE MORE THAN A CUP

### Orange-Ginger Chocolate Truffles

*One 2-inch piece of ginger, peeled and thinly sliced*
*2 ounces freshly squeezed orange juice, strained*
*Zest of 1 orange*
*2 ounces light corn syrup*
*8 ounces cream*
*8 ounces delicious bittersweet or semisweet chocolate, coarsely*
    *chopped*
*Cocoa powder for dusting*

Combine the ginger, the orange juice and zest, and the corn syrup in the cream. Bring to a simmer, then remove from the heat and cover. Let the ginger and zest steep for 15 minutes. Gently reheat the cream to just below a simmer and strain it over the chocolate. When the chocolate is soft, whisk it to combine it with the cream. Refrigerate the ganache until it's set. Using your hands, roll the ganache into balls of whatever size you wish and roll them in the cocoa powder to coat them completely. Refrigerate the truffles until ready to serve.

YIELD: ABOUT TWO DOZEN 1-INCH TRUFFLES

## *Basic Caramel Sauce*

For a caramel sauce, sugar is melted and cooked to an amber brown, then cream is whisked into it until the mixture is smooth and uniform. Two ingredients that don't taste particularly exciting on their own or together can be otherworldly when cooked and combined.

There are two ways to melt sugar, dry and wet. For dry, sugar is melted alone over low heat. For wet, just enough water is added to achieve a texture sometimes referred to as wet sand; I find it easier to control the browning of the sugar with this method. In both cases, use a large heavy-bottomed pot—enameled cast iron is perfect for the job— and one big enough that the caramel won't bubble up and overflow when the cream is added. The sugar should not be stirred until it's dissolved, though you can tilt the pan to make sure it heats evenly. Once the sugar is liquefied and has begun to brown, watch it carefully (once it's burnt, it can't be fixed). Also, be very careful—sugar is extremely hot and once it hits your skin, it stays there. Sugar burns are among the worst in the kitchen, so cook sugar carefully and thoughtfully.

Once the sugar has reached a dark amber color, remove it from the heat and add the cream (it will begin boiling immediately and vigorously; you can reduce the splattering by heating the cream first). Whisk continuously until the cream is completely incorporated.

I like to finish the sauce with butter for flavor and richness. For variations, the cream can be increased for a sauce that's pourable when it's cold. It can also be reduced for a very thick, rich sauce or for simply making caramels or toffee. The cream can be flavored with a spirit or a juice or infused with a vanilla bean for variations on the basic sauce.

*1 cup sugar*
*1 cup cream*
*4 ounces unsalted butter (1 stick; optional)*

Heat the sugar and just enough water to begin dissolving the sugar, a few tablespoons or so, in a large heavy-bottomed pan over medium heat. When the sugar is dissolved and beginning to brown, stir the sugar to ensure even cooking. When it is a beautiful dark amber, remove it from the heat and whisk in the cream, followed by the butter, if using. It will keep, well covered, in the refrigerator for up to a month. Reheat to serve.

YIELD: ABOUT 1¼ CUPS

## Old-Fashioned Butterscotch Sauce

Butterscotch has been so abused by the processed food industry (butterscotch bits, instant butterscotch pudding), few of us know why it's so special. It is an amazing sauce more people should make at home, since you can't buy it and few restaurants serve it. It's delicious over the Maker's Mark ice cream (page 213). Shuna Fish Lydon, who makes butterscotch as a pastry chef in San Francisco and writes about it on her blog, www.eggbeater.typepad.com, told me, "It's hard to explain getting the seasoning correct, but it's all about how the vanilla extract and the salt interact with the big sweet mass. Make a banana split [page 225] one night for your kids and have that around as a sauce. That's how it was first used in America."

*4 ounces unsalted butter (1 stick)*
*8 ounces dark brown sugar*
*8 ounces cream*
*1 teaspoon vanilla extract*
*2 teaspoons apple cider vinegar*
*½ teaspoon salt, or to taste*

In a heavy-bottomed saucepan or an enameled cast-iron pot, combine the butter and sugar over medium heat and cook until the sugar has melted completely and the mixture has taken on a thick frothy appearance, "lava-like," as Shuna aptly puts it, 5 to 10 minutes. Turn off the heat. Whisk in the cream until it's thoroughly incorporated. Let it cool for 10 minutes, then add the remaining ingredients. Taste and adjust the seasoning.

YIELD: ABOUT 1½ CUPS

## The Best Banana Split Ever

Because you did everything except grow the banana and milk the cow. Because you can't buy it anywhere—not like this. Because butterscotch and bananas are an *amazing* combination. Because this is like eating two or three desserts, but you can say it's just one. Because there is not a more quintessential American sundae anywhere. Created in 1904 by a twenty-three-year-old pharmacist in western Pennsylvania, the banana split is an ode to innocence and excess.

> 1 recipe crème anglaise (page 211), frozen in an ice cream
>   machine
> 4 ripe bananas
> 1 recipe butterscotch (page 224), warm
> 1 recipe ganache (page 221), warm
> 4 ounces cream, whipped to stiff peaks with 2 tablespoons sugar
> 4 to 8 maraschino cherries

Scoop portions of ice cream into 4 bowls (or 6 or 8). Split the bananas down the middle (and halve them if you wish) and arrange ½ to 1 banana per bowl. Pour about 2 ounces each of the butterscotch and chocolate sauce over the bananas and ice cream. Top with a dollop of whipped cream and a cherry.

YIELD: SERVES 4 TO 8

### Toffee

I love crunchy, caramelly sweet toffee at Christmastime, a decadent confection. It was years after I first made it that it dawned on me that toffee is simply the caramel sauce ratio, replacing the cream with butter. This recipe will give you plain toffee, but most often it's made with almonds and chocolate. If you wish, spread a single layer of slivered almonds on the bottom of a 5- to 7-inch baking dish and pour the hot toffee over them. Cover the top with 4 to 6 ounces of chopped chocolate. The almonds will cook and the chocolate will melt for a traditional crunchy English toffee preparation.

*8 ounces unsalted butter (2 sticks)*
*8 ounces sugar*
*1 teaspoon vanilla extract*
*½ cup slivered almonds (optional)*
*4 to 6 ounces chocolate, coarsely chopped, or chocolate chips*
  *(optional)*

Combine the butter and sugar over medium heat. When the butter has melted, add the vanilla. Cook, stirring, until the sugar has melted and the mixture has taken on an appealing toffeelike color. Pour it into a 5- to 7-inch baking dish (over the almonds, if using, and cover with the chocolate, if using).

# Epilogue

## The Ultimate Meaning
## and Usefulness of Ratios

My impulse to write books originates in the urge to find out what I don't know. Often I've heard people utter the words, "I've got a book inside me," or an idea to that effect, and it perpetuates an inaccurate view of how books are written. Often people who say they have a book in them are suggesting that if only they had the time to write down what's there inside them, they'd have a book. But the truth is, I don't think any writer sits down, opens up a faucet, and lets a story drain out into the container of their computer. The fact is, the act of writing generates the story. This is why it's so hard to sit down and stay down long enough to write.

For me writing is first and foremost an act of exploration and then creation. I wrote *The Making of a Chef* to find out what the most prominent school in the country said you had to know in order to be a chef. I wrote *Walk on Water* to find out who you become if, for your day job, you cut into and stitch up the hearts of sick babies. Cookbooks are no different, in my case. I didn't write *Charcuterie: The Craft of Salting, Smoking and Curing* because I knew all there was to know about it and wanted to tell others. I wrote it because I knew little about it and wanted to know more. The motive to write this book was the same. For a dozen years I've been infatuated with Uwe Hestnar's ratio chart. He wrote it to teach his students, lost in recipes, to get their heads out of books and to start cooking. To me, though, Hestnar's ratio sheet was an attempt to pare away all that was extraneous in cooking so that we could know what was fundamental. At what point did a pie dough stop being a pie dough and become a cookie dough? If we knew that, then we would truly know what pie dough was. He had reduced the hollandaise to two ingredients, yolk and butter, nothing else. Hollandaise has other ingredients—lemon juice, salt, and so on—but remove those and you still had an emulsified butter sauce. Take away the butter or yolk, however, and it ceased to be one.

What he was attempting, it's just now occurred to me, during this act of writing this morning, was *to create a Periodic Table of the Elements for the Kitchen*. What a brilliant idea. In an era when cooks are drifting, lost on a Pacific Ocean of recipes, this was landfall.

Could you really do this? Could you really get to the bottom of the entirety of cooking? This was what I didn't know but what I wanted to find out.

Well? What did I find out? I now know a lot about pediatric heart surgery and a lot about curing pork products. What do I know now that I've explored these ratios?

The most important thing I've learned in exploring ratios is the inter-connectedness of all our preparations. This is especially true of the dough-batter continuum, which is why it's meaningful to create a chart of it. Understanding a pasta dough helps you to understand a bread dough and a cookie dough and a pie dough better by recognizing what the variations, whether egg, water, or fat, do to the flour.

The second most important thing I've learned is how much cooking technique matters. I make a better pie dough than my photographer wife, even though we use the same ratio, because I've made more of them and so my fingers know how to knead the dough, just so much, just until it comes together, to achieve a flaky piecrust. "You didn't always make great pie doughs, just remember that," Donna said, miffed, when I was helping her to make one. In other words, care, observation, thoughtfulness, and, most of all, practice are every bit as fundamental to a preparation as know-ing the ratio.

Some ratios aren't as important as knowing what *is* important. I have made a stock ratio, 3 parts water to 2 parts bones, but it will still be stock if you use a 2 to 1 ratio. Recognizing why all the ingredients have to be submerged in order to be useful, though, is more important. Here ratios are useful guides.

Ultimately, ratios make cooking easier and more comprehensible because, as Hestnar's students discovered, when you knew the ratio, you didn't have to be chained to a book or a recipe.

On Sunday we invited some neighbors for dinner. While at the grocery store that afternoon, I figured I'd better make something sweet for after dinner. The easiest ratio I know is for cake, pound cake—equal parts butter, sugar, eggs, and flour. I usually reduce everything by half, to 8 ounces each. But to make sure I had enough, I figured I'd up everything to 12 ounces—which I could do because the ingredients are measured by weight. The cake came together almost without my having to think about it. It was mixed and in the oven 15 minutes after I got home. If I wanted only a couple of portions, I could have reduced it to 4 ounces.

Ratios liberate you—when you know the ratio and some basic techniques, then you can really start to cook.

# Acknowledgments

Michael Pardus and Bob del Grosso, chefs I met while at the Culinary Institute of America, read and commented on the manuscript throughout its writing. They were always available for discussion and advice, and their insights have enriched this text. I can't thank them enough for the time and thought they put into this book.

Cory Barrett, pastry chef of Lola in Cleveland, was enormously helpful in commenting on the doughs and batters. Susie Heller and David Cruz, chef de cuisine of Ad Hoc in Yountville, CA, also made valuable comments.

The above are chefs and colleagues and I'm grateful to them. A source of help that I hadn't expected came thanks to the Internet. While working on this book, a cooking site called Cook's Korner (www.cookskorner.com) invited me for a Q&A session while I was promoting my last book, *The Elements of Cooking*. The site is a place where committed home cooks share their experiences, ask questions, and give answers. A number of the members of the site asked if they could help me test recipes. I said sure and ultimately asked seven of them to help—this book is intended foremost for the home cook, after all. Gordon Anderson, Steve Baker, Matthew Kayahara, Dana Noffsinger, and James Wrightman were all extremely helpful. So was Chad Ward, author of an excellent guide to kitchen knives and knife skills called *An Edge in the Kitchen*. Skip Kennon, a composer and lyricist in Manhattan, was an eager and enthusiastic tester and commenter and I am especially grateful for his help. Marlene Newell, of Ontario, Canada, founded the site. She's been nothing short of heroic in her efforts to coordinate, monitor, and record the testing of every recipe in the book by these home cooks. She's a pro, and I'm truly grateful for her work.

As always, I must thank my friend and agent, Elizabeth Kaplan, and my fearless editor, Beth Wareham. My wife, Donna, went above and beyond in her attempts to capture the texture of food in black-and-white images.

Everyone, thank you.

# Index

Note: Page numbers in **bold type** refer to recipes.